ALL MY HEROES WERE HO'S

Copyright 2012 by Phyllis-Serene

Brown Skin Publishing

ISBN-13: 978-0971905733

ISBN: 0-9719057-3-8

Cover design: Michael Bronson grafik.hustle@gmail.com

Book design: CampbellsBookSoup.com

Photo credits: Copyright Phyllis-Serene unless otherwise noted

"I am one of those people who just can't help getting a kick out of life— event when it's a kick in the teeth." Polly Adler

Acknowledgments

To you, for the courage to pursue your personal truth. When we look beyond that which we are told is truth, we find that which is our own.

In my life, I've had many gifted mentors and friends that have made my path joyful, because I respect your privacy and safety I won't name each of you. I will only write *thank you for making my life come alive.*

For the lucky few who live "out," I hope to celebrate your unique beauty and intelligence with respect. Anything else would be an "oops," and we really hate those in the dungeon.

Foreword

by Rev Mel

There are times we wish we could touch life and really say what's on our minds. Phyllis-Serene does that in this amazing book with the insight of thinking out of the box. In her own words, she expresses what it's like to think like a woman of knowledge and passion with erotic imagination. The sexual potency of her words leaves you hungry for more as she takes you to the true place of eroticism, with an enhanced sense of womanliness. She is fearless as she shares her forbidden feelings and as she opens up herself to reclaim the sexual frenzy that possesses her soul. She brings out the Ho within you as you dance with her in All My Heroes Were Ho's.

Serene shows us that we can have ownership of our bodies and minds as she ignites symbiotic oneness with her heightened libido and unbroken ground of erotic taboo. Her words describe openness to the reality of lust and the sexual spirit. Even as a child she was consciously aware of her desires that she shares here. Her words give you the power of permission to explore a sexual revolution within yourself, and she invites your mind to release forbidden thoughts of the BDSM and kink journey. She gives you access to the wonderful and colorful interior of a life that some only dream of, but few have lived. Phyllis-Serene is a woman of many talents and a lexicon of human emotions as she runs naked with in these pages and allows you to come with her on the sexual adventure of a lifetime.

CONTENTS

Getting into Alignment

When I was a little girl, in between wishing for the handsome boy to kiss and marry, I prayed for wisdom. And I was one of those annoying kids that asked "why" a lot. You know, the kind that challenge you with questions until you run out of answers and reply with the age-old standard, "Because I said so!" That curiosity has been both a welcomed gift and driving taskmaster. It's kinda like being a human hound dog, always sniffing.

Guy Baldwin is the author of the BDSM classic, Ties That Bind. Guy is a frequent presenter across the country, and one evening my then-husband and I had him over for dinner. For Guy's evening entertainment, we invited a smart and, of course, hot young man over for the opportunity to sit at Guy's feet and learn from one of our Leather leaders. I am a Southern woman after all, raised to make sure to please all the senses when entertaining guests.

I sprinkled myself generously with some Domestic Goddess dust and labored to prepare freshly butchered steaks, organic veggies, and lavender crème brulee, and brought out the Canadian Ice Wine for the evening.

During dinner Guy shared one of those nuggets of wisdom he is revered for:

"When you look to develop a relationship, you need to align with your partner in five areas:

Spiritually
Intellectually
Emotionally
Instinctually
Sexually

Most couples connect in two areas and then wonder why the relationship didn't work out."

It reminded me of Barbara DeAngelis' work in the 80s about being partially matched with a partner. But more importantly, I realized that before we can connect with someone else, we need to get in alignment within ourselves.

We get out of alignment when our spiritual beliefs don't match our intellectual knowledge, for example, creation vs. evolution. Or, we've been raised with sexual beliefs that conflict with our spiritual, emotional, and instinctual intelligence, like the Madonna - Whore complex.

This book is the beginning of an exploration of my own getting into alignment. About half of the posts are from my blog, <u>Sin Like You Mean It</u>. I started the blog while in grad school at Antioch University. My neighborhood liberal college gave me space to think in print about the powerful, healing, and emotive experiences from my kinky view of the world.

I know if you and I sat down for a cup of tea, we could find more things in common than not. My goal is to help you get in alignment by sharing what I've learned.

Some stories I hope will take two hands to read, and some will challenge you. I hope both experiences will give you wisdom.

Who Is Serene?

I am often asked about how I chose a name for my kinky identity. Many of us select a scene name first because of the fear of exposure, but we also want that name to express personality, sexual needs, play styles, and goals.

My gay and lesbian friends have an advantage over kinky people in this major area: for them, coming out wasn't a name changer. Kink was an additional descriptor, but not their identity. (In no way am I attempting to address the painful and often forced way many have experienced coming out.)

Within our community, coming out is still a distant looming challenge. We still risk loss of family, job, and/or custody of children. There is little legal, religious, academic, or even kink community support. Declaring you are a sexual radical or kinky pioneer, or choosing a typically derogatory label like "slut" has a different impact than saying "Hi, I'm Bill, and I'm gay."

When I say "Hi, I'm Serene" it's my affirmation. It does not identify my sexuality, play style, favorite position, lusts, or self-imposed ranking with a title. It does identify, however, a sentiment rarely expressed in a quick introduction - my goals in my vanilla[1] and kink life.

I chose Serene based on an Aboriginal novel I read years ago. In the novel, the adults in the tribe, as part of their coming of age rites, chose a name based on a personality trait they were striving for. I started using alternative names (such as "Venus") in the 70s when going out to bars for the purpose of being a Cosmo Girl and getting my one night-stand on. Then, in the AOL chat rooms I was "Miss Spank U"; the adult chat rooms brought out names that identified the play I wanted to pursue.

At the time I chose "Serene," I identified as a submissive, (yes, I started with a 50 Shades of Grey lust, too), I was trying to balance my balls-to-the-wall career climb in the vanilla world with my sex life in a small town. I embraced my affirmation and committed to making it a life goal. When I added different monikers, e.g., "Mistress" or "Sadistic," mixing the word visuals amused me.

When choosing a name consider this: if you should be at a party and someone has to get your attention from across the room, will you remember the name you chose for yourself? When they compare the online representation to the real thing, how accurate will it be? The Internet gives us a false veil of protection. Does your name portray your desires, fantasies, and realities?

If you like calling yourself "Bitchy Sadist," "Killer Dom," or "sub-nothing," remember that strong words that invite judgment before people get the chance to know you.

My goal is still to be authentic to myself. Each day as I get comfortable living "out," I realize the voyage of acceptance and openness to share my experiences are welcomed. *National Coming Out Day* and the *It Gets Better Campaign* remind me that I can be Serene, or at least laugh trying.

Out of the Kink Closet

November 16 is the anniversary of my "Oops." In the dungeon we have a saying: "There's two things you never want to hear your Dominant say to you: 'Oops,' signaling something is wrong, and 'RED,' meaning something is really the freak wrong and stop immediately!" My vanilla "Oops" was a beautiful twist of irony that opened the door for me to come out of the kinky closet.

Like most American Kinksters and Fetishists, my kink practice was behind closed bedroom doors, and I kept up my vanilla life with work, community, church, etc.

On one hot summer day in 2005 I sought direction and received permission from the city and federal agency officials to whom I reported to allocate funds to my employees and myself that were earned from a federal grant. All good until three years later, when I blew a whistle (yep, in writing) on the City auditing staff. That was my "Oops."

An attorney friend said to me at the time, "Federal regulations are written vaguely enough so if they want to get you, they will," and they did. I spent the next two years defending myself, burning through my retirement and savings and only surviving by a super rescue from my big brother, resulting in the case being dismissed.

So here's the irony: After a lifetime of keeping my kinky life secret, when that ordeal was done and my political life was over, I had no interest in going back into the kinky closet. What the hell for?

Now, it was a six-figure, rather comfortable closet. It held my writing career, my coaching business, my politicking, and my nonprofit work. It kept my condo paid for and two cars in the garage. I was comfortable living my vanilla lie. The lie was produced most Mondays around the water cooler. It would go like this:

Co-worker: "You look like you had a great weekend. What you do?"

Remembering the awesome weekend of kinky play, personal growth or emotional healing I would wipe the smile off my face and say: "Oh nothing much, just hung around the house."

I hid the emotional, spiritual, and intense sexual experiences, because I couldn't talk about any of my weekend and leave out the flogging, or explain the delightful power exchange experience of submission and Domination.

Lying to others and myself was soul killing, as it is to anyone. The lie seemed to protect me, and it did for a while. But I was protecting a lie for what? A political career in mid-level non-profit management. So much of my personal growth was coming from my experiences in the dungeon that going back to vanilla life was no longer an option.

As an American I believe I have a constitutional right to do what I want with my consenting partner behind my locked bedroom doors. I disagree with the current laws that do not allow me to give consent to receive or give a sexual pleasure through a spanking or other forms of play we engage in. I practice informed consent and I want to keep my right to it. And I mind when the religious write laws that rob me of my rights. It's narrow-minded and selfish, and causes me to live in fear of my government. That makes me sad for the country I love.

I worked, volunteered, enjoyed a monogamous marriage, had great friends, and gave nice parties. I went to church and still believe in God, probably more than you do. I was a celibate missionary for twelve years and found I'm now comfortable being both the Madonna and the Whore. The Madonna embraces spirituality, wisdom, and deep emotional sacrifice of self. The Madonna, in her story, gives us the lesson of watching your child die as one of the greatest sacrifices a parent bears for the good of

6

mankind. Sacrifice for the greater good is a noble model to follow, and even volunteering can give us the high of giving. Call it "Sacrifice Kink" if you like. The beauty of Sacrifice Kink is it's got an exhibitionist side that gets stroked. It all feels good, that's why we do it.

And the Whore simply has more fun. When she is comfortable in her sexuality, she is powerful. A woman comfortable in her skin carries herself differently. It's beyond the power of beauty alone. The whore knows her value and she takes pride in her accomplishments.

The Preacher and the Whore, however, have the most in common. Their relationship is symbiotic. As a missionary in the 80s for a traveling tent revival ministry, I observed that the attendance was highest when the topic from the pulpit was the sexual sins. The congregation was tantalized with new fantasies from the testimonials of the young attractive sinners highlighted for the evening. The whoring ways of sinners makes a convenient stereotype for the audience to fantasize about.

The Preacher/Whore represents the yin/yang that makes each work best. Each one needs the other to do their job. Journalists are thrilled when they find the two in bed together. We've seen it enough to not be surprised anymore, unless of course, it's your preacher.

As Shakespeare wrote, "the lady doth protest too much." To me, this refers to our propensity to point the finger of blame and shame when we relate to an inward desire. We point it out in others, shame them if we can, and then we secretly fixate on it. It's an unhealthy cycle but a popular one. And it seems to happen every time we embrace extremes in belief.

A gay co-worker shared with me about his time before and after coming out. He recalled that he was such "a shit to women" because he hated who he was and hated them for wanting him. When he came out, the self-hatred went away. Now it's my turn. Hi, my given name is Phyllis, and my scene name is Serene, and I'm Kinky.

At What Age Did You Awaken?

In April 2011, I attended the Society for the Scientific Study of Sexuality conference with sexologists, sex positive academics, therapists, doctors, and practitioners. They got me to thinking about the first time I connected kink with sex. The conference affirmed what I knew from experience: kink experience can extend beyond the basic fulfillment of sexual pleasure.

I remember when I became awakened to kink while living on the island of Okinawa. The boondocks, or local jungle, held many hidden treasures to be discovered between the typhoons and the daily downpours. This was back then when it was safe to let kids explore on their own.

One afternoon I came upon a 12x12 one-room cinder block building. It had openings for doors and windows, but held neither. Inside the simple empty room were large rings mounted on the floor, ceiling, and each of the walls, about a foot above my head. I peered into the room from the doorway, carefully listening for the sound of adults ready to pounce on me. But all I could hear was the sound of my heart beating wildly and the blood rushing to my ears. I was excited and aroused by the adventure and the chance for discovery. I could feel the flush of blood coursing to the surface of my skin, and a throbbing ached in my lower torso.

It started to rain again, so I stepped into the empty room. As I looked to the right and left of the door, I saw images of naked women tied up in various positions with rope. They were red and black calligraphy strokes made by a careful artist. The beauty of the images held my attention through the storm. Years later I learned the room was dedicated to the art of Shibari. A room in the wilderness for surrender, freedom, bondage, and beauty in an environment where all exist together.

When the rain passed, I jumped onto my bike and headed home for dinner. The images firmly planted into my mind had warmed my body. And I was ravenous! I recall the taste of food was more alive in my mouth, and I asked for more vegetables for the first time in my young life. My taste buds were alive and craved satiation.

When bath time came, I found the warm water stimulated the continuing ache in my loins and then upon touch discovered my labia for the first time. Pleasurable throbs bolted through my legs and chest, along with a sweet pain of ache.

Now hold on, right there. You think you are heading for the masturbatory big finish, but this is not your average porn writer, this is Serene, your kinky to the bone, Sin Like You Mean It kinda writer. So now comes the interesting part of the story:

Baby Dildo

This was all new territory, and it never occurred to me there were holes in my body other than for excrement. With the assistance of gravity and my mother's vanity full of bobby pins, I began to discover what lies within. The bobby pins held my little labia lips in place with just the slightest tweak of pain and pleasure. And lo and behold there were three holes, not just two and all of them when stimulated created a most wondrous sensation. It was like discovering you loved broccoli and couldn't get enough of it.

Then I remembered the Japanese bondage room, where pleasure, beauty, and bondage all came together. And my little fingers found their way to combining that sensual memory with the ability to create my first orgasm experience. I was hooked, cementing sexual pleasure with the awe of discovery and understanding. My first fetish was born. I was five years old.

All My Heroes Were Ho's

Catholic schools fucked me over when it came to defining what *a professional woman was*. In the 70s, when the Women's Rights Movement had filtered down a message that I had to do something different than what my mother and the church told me was right, I looked for new role models. I searched for women I could relate to, aspire to be, and model after. Someone who made her own way in the world with money and a career, whatever that was.

But in 1974, my school was the Madonna/Whore Complex training academy and the first critical place I began to see life out of alignment. There were few models for a skinny, nerdy, black kid in those long, shapeless aqua-blue jumpers. The color matched the robe of the six-foot Blessed Virgin Mary statue that dominated the entrance of the school. And she was standing on a snake.

On television Diahann Carroll made the historical career move to nurse, a promotion from the maids I had witnessed in the past. But since I was squeamish around body fluids, so I headed to the library to see what history could teach me about successful working women.

Underneath my jumper a strong sexual appetite was in place. I was looking for women who could relate to what I was feeling, a stirring of their loins. I hoped the public library would satisfy my curiosity. After a couple of hours of research, I took the most explicit sex books I could find to the check-out counter. The elderly librarian took one look and said, "Honey those books are too old for you." And she stripped me of everything but a couple history books.

Grumbling and frustrated, I rummaged through my parents' stack at home. I found Polly Adler's *A House Is not a Home.* Adler was a twenty-year-old immigrant entrepreneur in Chicago. Her chosen industry: prostitution. I was hooked. Really, you could make money having sex. Tell me more.

She explained, "Prostitution exists because men are willing to pay for sexual gratification, and whatever men are willing to pay for, someone will provide."

She retired at 44 and refused to testify against her financiers, who then paid for her college education for her loyalty. She wrote her best seller and retired off the proceeds. Adler was a successful sex worker, with a famous retirement plan. Her non-fiction *how-to* was full of sex, power, and money with danger and glamour to boot! Now that's a career worth getting out of bed for every day.

I grew up hearing of this glamorous woman named **Josephine Baker** who left the United States in the 20s and became the most famous Black topless dancer, singer, and courtesan in the world, one of the first African-American women with star power. Baker, whose male and female lovers are estimated to have been in the hundreds, also managed to squeeze in being awarded the French Medal of Honor for being a World War II spy for her adopted country. That many lovers and save your country, too, that's a pretty high bar to set. She later adopted a dozen children from around the world, calling them her "Rainbow Tribe." In a game of Holy Poker, I think Josephine Baker beats Mother Teresa.

Pearl S. Buck taught me about the complexity of relationships with serial love affairs. She was a successful and prolific writer, winning the Pulitzer Prize in 1932 and the Nobel Peace Prize for literature in 1938, and a great humanitarian. Born the daughter of Chinese missionaries, it is not surprising that in 1917 she married Mr. Buck, a Southern Presbyterian missionary to China. Early into her marriage she started an affair with a Chinese poet. But the Boxer Rebellion ended that affair and forced Buck and her special-needs daughter back to the United States without her husband.

When she left China, Buck described how she felt as "a curious sense of pleasant recklessness," because though she had lost all her family's possessions, she was strangely free of her former life and its entanglements. Another affair followed, with her smart and ambitious publisher. With the success of her novel *The Good Earth*, Pearl had the career clout to divorce Mr. Buck and marry her publisher. They maintained an open marriage and, after her husband died, she graduated to Cougar status.

A creative humanitarian, Buck was outraged by the bigotry and abuse of mixed-race children left behind by American soldiers. She started the Pearl S. Buck Foundation that continues to support and brings these mixed-race children to the United States. [2]

Buck's writings demonstrate a depth of passion that shaped my view of love in the world. She taught me to believe in loving and deeply-involved complex relationships between lovers and religious and cultural expectations.

Another woman who owned her sex worker life and made history: **Mata Hari**. An exotic dancer, courtesan, and accused spy, she died at the hands of a German firing squad. Hari took the idea of making her passion her profession pretty seriously. You gotta admire a woman who becomes a heroine for her country through her passion.

Catherine the Great was known as the enlightened despot and a patron of the arts, especially if the artist was young and hot. She was a buxom woman known for her "hearty lust." Because of her, I became an art collector and artist lover.

And I can't forget the women of the bible:

In **Esther** we learn how to use feminine charm to snag a king. I call her the Patron Saint of Sugar Babies. With the help of her uncle, she saves her people, she though brutally and publicly destroys her enemies "Mexican Cartel" style. This sister was definitely from the hood!

Lot had a special father/daughter(s) relationship that made the writers of the Old Testament juggle with incest in the cleverest way. Look at Leviticus 18: the list of all the close relatives you can't have sex with. But guess what combo is missing? That's right, the father/daughter combo. Clever horde of holy writers, don't you think? But somehow the daughters get all the blame. I wonder how old these girls really were. How many news stories have you heard of daughters ganging up and getting their dad drunk to have sex with them?

These girls are survivors of incest. Their story is not told, and the Leviticus authors wrote this sin of omission, which provides a loophole for fathers who abuse their daughters. Their voice may be silent, but I see them and remember them as victims.

Now for the Grand Domme of all times - Stage Mother Extraordinaire - **The Blessed Virgin Mary** of course! She prepared, nurtured, and gave witness to a legacy for her entire family. She also gets credit for being the namesake to the most damaging role model for women ever: the barefoot Madonna. To me that image screams hippie, free loving kind of chick, and I was digging her. She was definitely Bad Ass, stepping on snakes—that's kinky.

Moving back to contemporary time, we have Saint **Oprah's** arrival in the 80s. I admire Ms. Winfrey for staying single and maintaining a lasting relationship. I believe her story deconstructs the Madonna/Whore complex. As a single woman, Oprah lives the Whore life, shacking up for years without the cultural approval of marriage and wildly profitable while serving as the Madonna to half of humanity with her work. It's through her story we see that both archetypes can work together successfully. I hope that when her story is told from history's perspective that her personal life will part of the legacy, along with her career. Black women have the furthest to climb to reach success. Oprah is the Superior Black Domina.

These *Heroes* set pretty high standards, made tons of money, and had fun being their sexual selves. Through them, I could envision a path that would allow me to use my brains, passion, compassion, family, beauty, and sexual drive to forge a memorable life.

Go Ho's! You Rock!

Roses for Scars

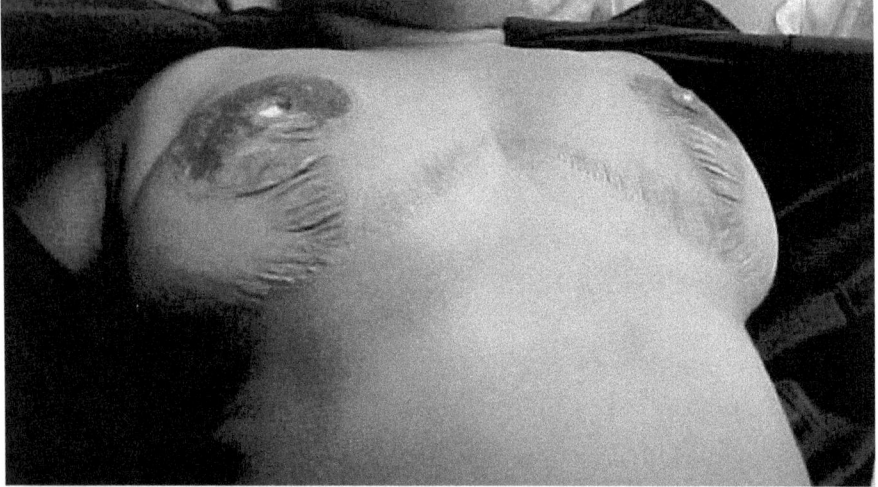

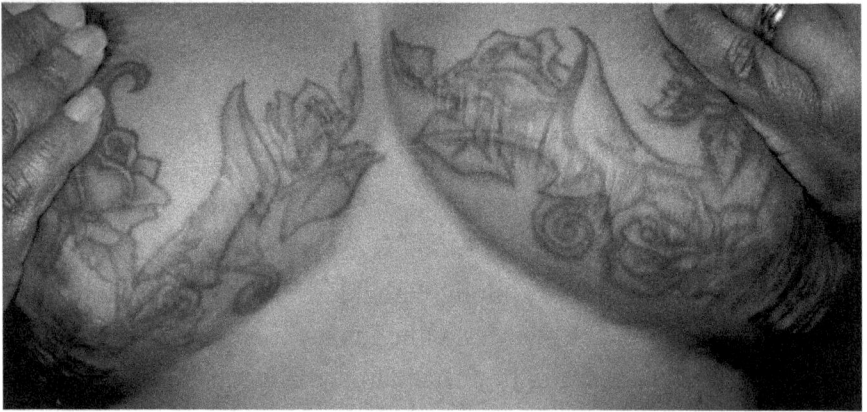

I don't think I'm the typical body mod story, but today I don't think there is a typical story. The only tattoos I recall were the stacked brunette on my Dad's arm from his years in the Air Force and his ability to make her hips move in a suggestive walking manner. I thought that was great fun and thought all tattoos were just an extension of male sexuality. Well, at least until I thought of getting my own a few years ago.

In 1998, I had eight pounds of fat, tissue and skin removed from my breasts. This extra weight caused me to get saddle shoulders and though my 5'10" frame looked in proportion, I didn't feel it. I was the girl that always got the breast man, but for the life of me, I couldn't find anything attractive about my triple D cups. It was a nice touch to mention them in online dating scenarios, but in reality, outside the cup was not so pretty. Picture nipples reaching down to my navel and you're close, and I had not turned thirty-five yet.

I spent the next six months looking for plastic surgeons skilled in breast reductions. When I finally settled on one, the day of the surgery I went into a panic right as the doc was using his Sharpie to mark the cuts, and said. "Wait, I don't want a C-cup, I might miss the sisters. Give me just a single D-cup." So the Doc re-marked me and away I went for hours of surgery.

Three days later, when I finally was alert enough to check my bandages, I noticed leakage on my right side and got a friend to help me take a peek. Somehow my nipple had torn and I had a new two-inch gash, and now a lop-sided breast. I went back to the doctor pissed off, and he offered to do another surgery at my expense, which pissed me off even more, but I had to wait for it to heal before he would go back in. I waited another three agonizing weeks, watching the scars take hold of my right breast, causing the nipple not only to tear but also to be more sensitive than the left one. So, imagine a circle with 65 percent of it cut out and smashed down into the rest of the tissue. When it's cold the left nipple looks normal, but the right only has 35% of it standing at attention.

I watched the rest of my body heal over the next few weeks and hated all the scars I saw every day in the mirror. I felt like Frankenstein's Bride. One evening I was watching a Discovery Health show where a woman had covered her double mastectomy scars with a beautiful, colorful midriff top made entirely of tattoos. She would go into the locker room of her gym and women would come up to her and comment on the beautiful work, and then after a while notice she no longer had breasts. I thought how clever that the beauty of the work made people forget what was missing. I thought that would be the perfect solution for me.

I found my tattoo artist after seeing a short piece in the *Wall Street Journal* about a female artist. She designed fifteen roses in various states of bloom (seven on the left, eight on the right) to gracefully cover the scars, fill in the tears, and outline the nipples. The process took a few weeks to finish. I spent Sunday afternoons in a private room getting to know all about the world of tattoos, though I never got to see anybody else get theirs done. And I was surprised how little pain there was. The scar tissue had deadened the skin and only at the breastbone and underneath the arms was the tattoo work painful.

I have since had cancer and have thought about another tattoo to cover my port-a-cath scar, but I'm still wincing at the memory of the pain. The before and after pictures I hope you will agree were worth the effort! I have since become a big fan of the art and am considering going back for at least a touch up of the nipples. The ink has faded, which surprised me since they rarely get sun on them. Nevertheless, that's my story and I'm sticking to it.

New Year Sobriety

I owe my sobriety to the first leather event of the year, a funeral for a fine woman I knew in the lifestyle. We were a mix of people sitting in the pews, leather folks, the AA community and her extensive family. Hearing her friends share her life from their perspective revealed a common experience: her character was defined by her spoken word, her work to support fellow alcoholics, and a living example of a polyamorous submissive, working to make her family a welcoming place for family and friends, especially hungry ones who appreciated her fine cooking.

And she was one of the lucky ones, who lived mostly *out* in her lifestyle choices. The program leaflet identified her community of friends in the leather lifestyle, which easily represented a third of the mourners in attendance. I made my condolences to her mother, who connected the stories of the corsets her daughter made for me.

This was my first leather funeral and I couldn't help but put myself in the coffin and in the picture on the cover of the program, and listen to the words of friends who knew me well. I wondered who would attend and speak on missing my life and what it represented to them?

A week before her death, her last advice to me was to reflect on the past year and to look forward to what I wanted to or will do differently in the next. I typically look at life from the lessons learned and opportunities still ahead. In my leather life that means:

Fewer floggers and more medical supplies
Fewer corsets (I have twelve) and more books
Fewer fetish balls and more leather conferences
Less hanging out and more mentoring

Less focus on what I don't believe and more on what I do believe - Hedonism.

I am thankful for so many things and much less afraid of the future, despite the economy and our black socially conservative president. And I will strive to live each day in more honest love.

Happy New Year Cici, see you on the other side.

Shame Is a Masque

It's a blessing and a curse to need radical honesty in your life. It drives me to look inward and wrestle with the lies I tell others and myself. It makes my sexuality come on stage for display.

Remember the bible story of the guy wrestling with an angel all night to get his blessing? That's me; I'm a greedy girl, even if it costs me my hip or pain to get it.

Radical honesty has bit me in the ass when it comes to relationships. I'm still working on kindness first, with the critique sandwiched in the middle.

I recall the advice of one author to give five compliments before one criticism. I could never think of five, and when I was ready to criticize I couldn't think of one good thing. That made me more effective in keeping my mouth shut and weighing the value of my two cents.

As a practicing Quaker (Religious Society of Friends) that belief system has taught me that my internal wrestling works out the hell in this life so I don't face it afterwards. I can accept that belief as it mirrors the Buddhist, Hindu, and Judaic belief that we learn continually: we improve our lives individually, as a community, and as a planet as part of our evolutionary path. After all, we are all on this ball going around in circles together.

I've watched enough YouTube Kabbalah lessons to learn that mankind has to ascend together. Yikes, that's not good news for the individualist like myself, who selfishly focuses on getting mine and getting off this planet to the next place. But it also explains why our highest calling on the earth is to serve mankind. We all *gots* to go together!

Honesty makes me want to rip open my heart and expose it to the light. I want no corners of doubt, just the clarity of knowing I'm right. Yet,

21

with each step I take into uncertainty, doubt, and new places, I feel vulnerable, shy, and extremely turned on.

Boldness is the requirement for the entrepreneurial action. It is the base for our success soup. The risk taker's reward is success. But what about the woman who risks being honest in relationships? Her reward is an empty bed. Does that empty and honest bed feel good? Sometimes it does. The bed I share with a cub, lover, submissive, bottom, stranger, dominant, husband, or girlfriend always has a story, an adventure, and a lesson to be learned. And I love learning.

Creating paths for fantasy to be explored and experienced is my passion. How cool is that? Women have difficulty getting what they want because we don't ask for it; we hint instead.

Sadly, nobody tells the man he needs to be guessing more. Our nature is about looking out for the others in our lives. We make great Moms, Dommes, Nurses, and Teachers—always giving to others.

We have work to do, however, with getting our lovers, orgasms, and money. But when we do, we are successful, happier, and balanced. That combination of our sexual beauty and willingness to share that power is a moneymaking combination and the basis for the oldest profession. It is also the commerce of life for us. Men know our power, women flirt with power and religion, and the government controls that power in repressing both sexes and thus slowing down the evolution of the planet.

Making sense of all this is important for all of us. Clearing a path for us to reach and grasp higher and more sincerely moves us all toward the finish line of life. Life has a burden of death. But death is not the end, just a restart. We can work like the dickens in one life and loaf about in the next if we choose. But the lessons are the same for all mankind. And with the volume of humans that continue to fill the planet beyond its capacity to sustain itself, I wonder when the tipping point will be made clear to everyone.

I remember reading about a garbologist who said that when a society begins to worry about its trash, that's when it's too late. He wrote that in the 70s. I grew up watching the trash commercials of Keep America Beautiful and the tearful Indian viewing the destroyed lands at the hands of commerce and disregard for the ball we call home, and I sometimes call "prison," since it is really kinda hard to leave. A few escape and orbit for a while and come right back home. We're trapped here to figure out how to escape for good. We should work together on this.

I like working on the sexuality piece and getting that back into alignment. Part of that understanding begins when you remember you are a mammal. We have an animal nature and human learning. Our lessons have come from fables, religious beliefs, and now science.

Today there is plenty of research to show you how healthy your kinky sexuality is, how you can live a normal happy life with your play, improve your relationships, heal fears, banish the shame mask, and feel healthy and alive till the day you die. Leave the planet happy and ready to jump back on the ride again.

I Wish to Confess I'm a Cougar

I have a penchant for beautiful boy toys. I don't care if they are white, black, brown, or yellow; frankly, my cunt just sees the delightful sinews of flesh that hug ribs, six packs, glutes, and muscles groups I can't even begin to name but love to see working their magic in any performance.

And I'm delighted to welcome my Panda into my fold of friends. Don't look for him on the kink channels yet, as I'm hoarding him for myself for a little while longer. Call it the selfish delights of a curmudgeon. But 'I'll write about the parts of delight that stick in my head: the effortless laughter in play, the confidence that comes from perfecting a skill, and channeling skill into power as I've witnessed in his gambol.

I've always been fascinated by the art of the Geisha. They have the gift of entertaining solely for one's multi-level hedonistic pleasures - visually, musically, rhythmically, artfully, and passionately. The senses can be overwhelmed with all that is received from a Geisha, and in his case, a *Gaisha* who has finely developed at an early age those skills that make him desirable.

A delight to these mature eyes that have seen so much beauty. It continually captures the eye and loins to see youth, with grace and intelligence, precision and delicacy in a body. Youth is not wasted on the young!

Try New Compersion: Jealousy Be Gone!

Tired of those nagging jealous emotions you can't seem to shed? Ready for a new emotion? Then try the new and improved, emotional response called "compersion." It's so new it's not even in the Internet dictionary yet.

So why am I jealous? As a poly believing, free love kind of Leatherwoman, I practice and teach adults to explore their kink, fetish, or other expressions of expanded sexuality and loving. But that green monster can ruin a hot dungeon scene every time.

Jealousy has caused many of my relationships to crash and burn. I honestly don't know when love changes to possessiveness, but it does. After one ex-boyfriend decided to date my roommate, my response moved into violent attack mode. Thank goodness the internal rage also temporarily blinded me, so all I could literally see was red, and I was frozen in my tracks. That gave me time to think, calm down, walk away, and find a new place to live.

I would prefer another emotion than the one that beats up my heart and mind like a bronchitis attack. Jealousy has a way of kidnapping my time and energy in directions I don't want to go. I recall the rush of un-pleasant emotions that made my stomach knot up, my hand form a fist, words spew forth I would regret—all part of the cycle I wanted to break. But how could I break free of the green stain?

With the divorce rate in America comfortably above 50%, partnering for life is no longer the norm. I needed another emotion that could keep up with our societal change. At a polyamory meetup, I was introduced to the word: *compersion*, the antithesis to jealousy. Here's the Wiki on comper-sion:

"Compersion is a state of empathetic happiness and joy experienced when an individual's current or former romantic partner experiences hap-piness and joy through an outside source, including, but not limited to, an-other romantic interest. This can be experienced as any form of erotic or emotional empathy, depending on the person experiencing the emotion."

Nice concept, but the million-dollar question is, how can I be happy when MY old lover is loving someone else? Then I remembered the C.S. Lewis book, The Four Types of Love. Lewis defined the following types of love: agape, philia, eros, and storge. I've paraphrased his concepts:

Agape is the spiritual love you have that comes from your beliefs.

Philia is the bond of friendship.

Eros is the emotional intimacy we share in a relationship. (Venus is described as the "Fifth Love" and is the passion and energy of sexual ex-change, its trademark being a temporary state of experience, likc orgasm and infatuation.)

There is another more powerful love that helps to explain the ability to convert jealousy into compersion:

Storge is the familial love of parent to child. Storge can be more powerful than all the others combined. It's the type of love that gives a parent superhuman strength to lift a car to save a child's life.

Compersion suggests that if we can adjust our thinking, heal our emotions, we can celebrate our partner, lover, spouse, or ex's happiness in another relationship. We can replace jealousy with joy.

You also receive extra feelings of contentment and maturity with every use of compersion. Like when your child goes off to school for the first time or the last time, (hopefully) away to college. There is pride of being a part of making that success happen. And I like being a part of someone's success.

Jealousy can hold me in this knee jerk reaction of anger, hurt, and then retribution. By reminding myself that the experience has passed, I can change my thoughts. If that doesn't work, then I remember why the relationship needed to end in the first place and my head clears, fist relaxes and I can look for the good of this new coupling and let the joy of compersion build in me.

Now have I done it? Not every time, but I'm working on it. It's not like one day you wake up compersed. It's the *art of letting go* of past anger that takes time and practice. And when I have a surge of emotions that race up to my brain and fist at the same time, I acknowledge the emotion and look at it. I then look at where I want my emotions to be and go there. No need to replay the old tapes. My heart calms, pulse slows, teeth unclench, and I can think without anger. I take a deep breath, let compersion in, and make a choice to celebrate my (ex) lover's new relationship and wish them well. It's that simple and that difficult. But the end result is my joy and happiness and I'm definitely worth the effort.

The Varying Beauty of Leather Relationships

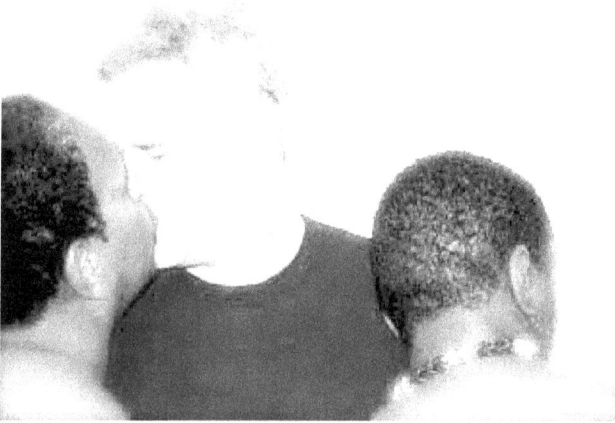

Kissing exhubby with Enoeny

My former husband and his new submissive and I were hanging around one weekend and I thought the coincidence of this pic would make a good topic for examination. Sooooo … while they were off in the bedroom getting their kink on, I wrote this piece about the unique qualities of being in a dual bi, kinky, double Dom, swinger positive, poly and open marriage …

I realize that alone could stop all other conversations at the Thanksgiving dinner table and it should. But dear kinkster, realize we all didn't wake up one day and decide we were kinky or bi or poly. We took our time and with each subsequent orgasm, when our creative juices flowed over us like Niagara Falls, we thought about ever increasing ways to increase our pleasure. And when pleasure is shared it has a wonderful bonding effect that, in our case, made our marriage of ten years work.

My husband and I met as kinksters, so we were half way to home base. We each had our own paths that brought us together. But the basis for the marriage was open communication, exploration, and a sense that life is about the journey, not destiny.

Don't get me wrong—the first few years of marriage we shared our home with the green monster of jealousy. But somewhere between living together, knowing each other, fighting the enemies within as well as without (illness, job loss, community gossip, jealous subs, etc.) we found within each other a strong support to lean on.

My response to the question of jealousy has been, "I have his heart and his wallet. His dick can go anywhere." Why? Because he and I both get to come home to love and acceptance. And that's still very hard to find out there anywhere, vanilla or kink, swing or poly.

Man has proven it is not a species that mates for life, though the constructs of our community, primarily through religious institutions, develop marriage as a contract that allows for social control. Marriages are hard pressed to survive under any pressure, let alone thrive year after year. The marriages that make it for any length of time do so because they share something of value. It could be the love, the kids, the money, the sex, or the comfort. If you are lucky you learn that the value you share is the love for each other. I was able to say goodbye to jealousy once and for all when I faced all the fears it brought up, discussed them, and then went forward trusting (and testing) the marriage commitment.

I came to marriage not because I needed a man, but because I wanted one. I wanted to share the journey. I suspected my life would be fuller with someone I could tell my wild stories to, eat popcorn and ice cream for dinner with, and lust after the same hot bodies over. What a dream come true, I was one lucky fucking bitch! And I enjoyed it, while it lasted.

Waves of Gratitude

I have an ocean theme flowing through my brain, feel the breezes coming through our southern California condo. My ex and I were privileged to publicly bestow a first piece of earned leather last night to a young man in service to us. This is an almost foreign concept these days in the age of "instant Masterdom," but a throwback emotionally for us old folks who remember the private meetings in homes, garages, and basements. Those clandestine parties were so needed and worth the risk of loss of family, friends, work, and reputation.

That time has passed and though I fight the use of the word "nostalgia," I can't help but remember that community of friends, one that came together out of necessity. With the advent of the Internet in the mid-nineties, we kinksters finally got off the farm, only to hide behind pseudonyms of screen names. I miss and wonder about those early friends.

So when bright minds, open spirits, and willing explorers came into our lives we were pleasantly surprised to find kindred hearts. But for some time the concept of leather family had not expanded in my own mind beyond the idea of a polyamorous relationship. Today, necessity due to financial, emotional, physical, or spiritual needs has opened a door of opportunity to create support for each other that includes a family dynamic that may look like a scene from "Mad Max" or "Waterworld," but is still an essential unit for my own growth as a human.

My wave of gratitude comes from the joy of pouring my own life's mistakes, experiences, and mutual desire for camaraderie into willing ears that have become close friends. I am proud of our leather family, and I am amazed they keep their heads when others have disassociated themselves mentally or emotionally from their kink. (That separation always feels like a slap in the face, and I don't like pain.)

These days I think and speak more about why we do kink instead of how. It's been a great opportunity to look at our lives and the choices we made professionally, many of us moving to live this life 24/7. I am who I am because of rejection and fear and then the grace to overcome and thrive. I don't run from the rejection any longer. I let those waves ride over me and know that with the good emotional release of a flogging or spanking I can ride this storm of life too. And when the waves come I'm ready, for I have family.

The Pursuit of Pleasure

I'm a sex geek. The Internet has kept me well fed with my addiction for the latest research on the natural sexual function of our bodies. The more knowledge I gain about how my body works, the more mini orgasms I get to experience. See why I love research? By sixteen, I had learned what parts gave me an orgasm and taught myself to manipulate my body to improve upon that pleasure.

My grad school friend Marya texted me one day and suggested that we go to Santa Monica Pier and ride for a few hours, saying, "I need to pump the feel-good juices up". Marya has learned to give herself alternative physical highs to the liquid ones that come in a bottle. Brilliant idea, and I was happy to be invited. I had just finished reading *Born to Be Good* by Dacher Keltner. His research examines the science of emotions. Not the cause of them, per se - but how emotions manifest in the body. I was looking forward to experiencing the rides from the perspective of what emotional manifestations would be created in my body.

It was a lovely spring afternoon on Santa Monica Pier. We jumped on four rides over and over again, and then watched the sun set over the Pacific Ocean. The Sea Dragon was our first ride. The long green canoe whips its passengers from one end to the other, forcing your body to swing forward and back, and though your stomach leaps, the swing feels controlled I carefully looked at the kids and adults before me in line for queasy faces that might lose their cookies on the Dragon. Seeing none, we headed for the last row of the dragon seats, assured we'd get the most intense ride and endorphins. As the Sea Dragon started its pendulum swing, I noted that the lift of my internal organs created a giddiness and then laughter that escaped from me as I experienced the tingling sensation throughout my upper torso. My heart was lifted, as if all the burden of weight had been released in each upward swing. The emotions were like an intense exhilaration and when the ride was done, a joy settled over me like a light dusting of snow. We walked away feeling cleared from the past burdens that brought us here, now tingling and itching for more.

The next ride was the Pacific Plunge, which takes riders seated five in a row up a single tower and then drops them again, forcing the weight of your organs to fly momentarily upward. The combination of the visual beauty of the Pacific Ocean, the approaching sunset, and the ride sealed in a pleasurable memory I knew I would have forever. My body felt like it was experiencing an upper body orgasm. The combination of joy, fear, exhilaration, beauty, and awe and their chemical roots—adrenaline, endorphin, oxytocin, and other pheromones—the body delivers beautifully. As my Mama would say to my constant questioning, "It just feels good, that's why." We filled up our emotional cup feeling buoyed by the experience and ready to take on the week ahead. I left understanding my body a little better, using the memory to reconnect to feelings of elation from that day.

So what happened? I used the physical stimulus from the one activity to fill an emotional need. The natural chemical highs from the rides were a healthy option to finding your joy in a bottle.

Marya and I at Santa Monica Pier

Kinky Living

I Love an Intellectual Challenge

Every now and then a single word will strike me as hot and then I get that little moisture release that feels so good even in the smallest dose. Like when a grown as man calls himself a *slut*. Why does that make me so wet? The word delivers to my mind's eye delicious, salty wetness. I love salty things, crave them more than the sweet kisses and sugary nonsense that has never has the good manners to pass the hips as it did so swiftly on the lips. But I digress.

I love how a single word instantly causes a reaction in those sub-coccal regions. We feel a depth of delicious when we want to dive down and look at that ever so tiny drop of pre-cum that we all have, which I'm afraid we do not release often enough. So let's celebrate the words or phrases that personally bring out our wetness, and follow them with a phrase that describes what picture comes to you. I'll start:

Slut - A warm tongue dancing up the inside of my thigh. Pant.

Your turn: _____ Say it out loud. Okay, but not too loud.

Top High

Some fantasies take longer to fulfill than others, but are well worth the wait when you get to them.

My early fantasies, I'm talking at six or seven years old, were about puncturing flesh. I wondered what the sensation would feel like and tried safety pins and sewing needles on myself. I found the pricks stimulating to my pre-pubescent clit and kept exploring. I know what you're thinking: she was a cutter trying to release her pain. I never heard of cutters until I saw the movie, *The Secretary*; I was just curious. You don't see cutters sitting alone in a dungeon, for that's a solo act of pain release, not play full of sexual energy. Once I had gone through the fantasy of puncturing, I was on to something else. It's the Sagittarian in me, always curious.

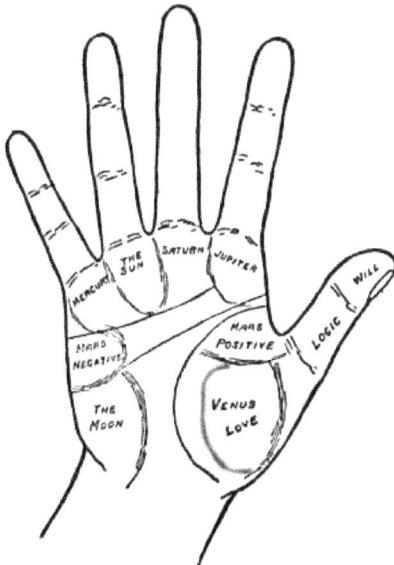

I found the same pleasures came from biting my Mount of Venus, loved how I could connect pain to pleasure and stimulate my gut and my loins throughout the day. Those bites had a calming effect too. Over the years I noticed calluses on my left hand from my continual chomping on my pleasure pacifier.

I timidly lost that needle pleasure when I first encountered needle play from Queen Cougar in 1998 in Ft. Lauderdale. I was there with my future husband, attending the Beyond Leather Conference. The Leather Community royalty were there in force, with Guy Baldwin and Vi Johnson. Cougar was then part of a triad of Black Lesbian Leather Women who were a Family. They are individually three Goddesses walking the earth, and when you saw them together, you immediately saw majestic powerful women, relaxed and comfortable in their skins.

2009: the hunger for puncture came back. I connected to it again at the DESIRE conference, watching blood splattered women come out of their rooms after intense orgasms with drunken smiles, which made me want that pleasure that has so often been associated with our female pain. This was blood flow that I could control and use for my cunt's pleasure. Queen Cougar was there to re-introduce me to the pleasure of piercings.

So when a lovely Canadian landed in my lap for play that evening in the Palm Springs desert and she had the same desire for blood play as a masochist -Kinky Nirvana. We have a match, let's play ball!

Delicately designed, primed, and trimmed of any unnecessary fat or hair, she was ready for the release of endorphins that needles can deliver. And when I placed a piercing just above her breast, the puncture went through energetically to me, connecting to my clit and delivering an electrical pre-orgasmic buzz.

But orgasms make me sleepy and I couldn't give myself the pleasure I wanted from her body to feed mine by letting our endorphins mingle in sexual embrace. Still, I was getting drunk. That's what Top-space highs are like: a bit like driving drunk.

My duty is to care for my play partner and ensure her safety, pleasure, and comfort while she's experiencing sub-space. But I am drunk too in the endorphin, oxytocin, and serotonin high, fighting to keep my hand from my crotch. I cross my legs and kegel the flows to maintain my state. Not that the crowd would mind if I stripped and came before them during intense public scenes, but I know I have miles to go before I can sleep.

The next day I was home and sitting in my car, waiting to calm down from the bridled pleasure I was still feeling from 72 hours of play. Then, the miracle occurred: my husband arrived home just as I got out of the car. He carried my toy bag upstairs as we shared stories of our separate play experiences from the weekend.

His was a gentler experience with rope bondage, spanking, and multiple orgasms with his new beautiful Creole submissive. "A gift from the leather gods," he calls her. Our stories came together in a timely manner. I retold mine and we finished the scene with our own extremely hot sex. BDSM is great foreplay for conventional sex.

We laughed in bed at the plight of our double Dominant challenge of getting off from our separate and divergent styles. It's a delicate dance that we have talked about with differing levels of success, and finally failure at making a Dom/Domme relationship work. But it sure made for some great shared memories.

Intuitions

I have of late begun to look more at the past than the future. I suppose it has something to do with age and fear of the future in these unstable times.

I believe the primary reason for growth is that it forces you to stretch neurons, emotions, and even physicality in new, unexpected, sometimes painful and joyful ways that are so fucking insightful you piss people off, you're so happy with your life.

There's a part of my body that has lain dormant for some time: my intuition. And like most humans, I have allowed my mind to talk me out of what my body has already come into agreement with and alerted me about. That learned habit I believe is one of the glitches in being human. We have a few glitches with genes going awry. Our intellect trips us up from being in our bodies. We get out of alignment. We, as kinksters, know that and work to bring the body and mind together.

Kinksters today can recognize, accept, and even celebrate what our bodies have longed for: Real Human Experience. We have all found a fetish or two, or 200, as an extraordinary means to meet an end. Many of us find kink a still shameful but addictive habit. But many more of us now understand that we have a choice in our sexual identity and relationship lifestyles. We have incorporated kink in our professions, ministry, politics, and art, thus getting back into alignment with a healthy expression of our sexuality.

I've come to understand that our choices are simply formed by our words. And our words are formed by our training and life experiences. Please stop speaking and manifesting what you fear. Better to *look* at the fear, for then you can choose another path.

Intuition will help you with that. It's that little gut twinge, the shortness of breath, the little death of fear, the emptiness of the lungs, and the anticipation. We use these stimuli in our play all the time, mimicking its effects on us like a drug. We can't get enough of it.

I would challenge you to look at when your own intuition begins to rise in your body. Notice it, look at it, listen to it, feel it, but don't deny it. Don't discount intuition; don't let your brain tell you a lie.

Listen to intuition during the flutters of pleasure; what is it saying to you then? I find I feel it on different sides of my solar plexus, and I'm trying to listen better to what my body is telling me.

Just remember, your organs all have brains and minds and they work in harmony with the rest of the body automatically—if we let them. This little human brain glitch can be overcome with awareness and practice.

Resolution—wrestle with the inner demons we call our conscious. It is our personal path toward ascension. We all have a need to escape even for the moment; we want to release the burden of honest toil for a bit of pleasure. I say *let's play*. Move the fantasies through our system, and give us the perspective that only comes from the other side of memory and experience. Sometimes we need to be bound to be free, like a swaddled baby needs to be comforted, returning back temporarily to the womb of safety.

The Fine Art of Endorphin Rushing

When my new yoga magazine came in one day, an ad caught my attention. The Shakti Mat is a smaller, portable Indian bed of nails that the advertisers say will "give you meditative relaxation, dissolve all sorts of tension and release endorphins and oxytocin."

Hmmm, I said to my kinky self, "I'm a Therapist!" At least, my goal in play is to release those same endorphins, but not so much oxytocin, since that is the love drug and I'm not looking for relationship building.

So what are these endorphins all about?

Remember runners' high, and that rush you get after a great cardio workout? Well, endorphin rushing is about that same goal, but it takes some exertion on your body's part (or by my hands) to reach it. That intense flogging that starts to make you sweat is all about releasing the endorphins to the body for its hard work. It's your body's way of saying *atta-a-boy*.

I have come to admire those needle play folks or "pin cushions" who can achieve their highs from the simple piercing of flesh. And I will admit I'm finally enjoying my childhood fantasies of piercing and cutting flesh and equally get a rush from the activity.

It's the high that BDSM has to offer. And I'm pleased to work and perfect my craft. Peace out.

More Adult Talk Please!

I must say that I enjoy talking to people about that secret kink they can finally admit to themselves, share it with someone, and then release the hold it has had on their lives. The sigh of relief that comes from simply sharing those hidden secrets removes shame, builds confidence, and allows you to feel more normal and wonderfully alive. That's what it's all about. It's not that their secret fantasy is all that dirty, crazy, or potentially shaming that is of interest to me, but the process you go through to get to them to the memory side is priceless.

In an honest conversation, the positive release of energy is shared, and that's what I like. It's when we act on our need to express these desires that the energy becomes powerful for both parties. It's even more powerful when you have a supportive ear on the other side. I call it Adult Talk and we need more of it.

I don't know when in your life the need to hide your sexual desires started, but my sexual interest started long before I heard the word "no," so I'm comfortable with expressing my desires for play, sex, and relationships and the freedom to pursue them.

Each step into mature adulthood is about acknowledging and respecting those desires within for sexual, emotional, mental, and physical needs of fulfillment. Of course I will add: "'within the confines of the laws and moral standards of your community." As a practitioner of BDSM, I have more opportunities to communicate creatively and practically with my mind, body, spirit, soul, and sexual expression of myself.

Natural High

Endorphin highs are like no other. Sending your bottom or submissive into subspace, I believe, is the real art of Domination. And when you can get that right mix of sadistic pain and pleasure, the result is delicious. When the two sensations create the chemical reaction of hybrid intensity that short circuits normal brain and body functions, the body begins to soar. Let me tell you about my Saturday night, and you can decide how close I came to soaring.

I always enjoy the company of a 3B (Black, Buff and Beautiful). I've waited for this particular 3B for some time and have looked forward to what his youth and vigor could sustain. This night he surprised me. I think you know by now that I love good sensual, sadistic play and love it even more when I can dance with a sensual masochist. I have the good fortune of playing with a couple of these darlings on a regular basis. It's good to be me.

Back to my 3B for the evening: I started with a body inspection. I always look for scratches, bruises, moles, discoloration, etc. Often single people do not have someone to do these close inspections and bring attention to areas that may become health issues. It's part of Safe, Sane and Consensual and *caring* play.

My 3B was ready to play, flaccid, but beautiful. I kept him in a room all to myself as I had no interest in sharing him or being distracted by other players or an enthusiastic audience. 3B's are always a feast to the eyes and this man was particularly built with six-pack abs and thunder thighs. Yowza!

After a sufficient warm up of spanking and some impact thumps I put on my vampire gloves and began to press into his flesh. He moaned as my hands moved about his body. Vampire gloves are embedded with sharp studs that are not folded down, but instead come through the inside portion of the glove so that using your palm and the undersides of your fingers on any surface (if used lightly) feels like a knife tip. Pressed harder, the glove feels like a vice grip of lightly blunted thorns trying to break skin.

Standing him on a platform, I stood behind him, instructed him to grip the bars in front of him to brace his body. With one side of the smooth glove I stroked his penis that had already started to rise from my earlier attention. I pressed my thumb down into his cock with my right glove, and then lifting his cock, I moved down to his ball sac. He made sounds of pure honey to my ears, and each prick of the glove had him humming and going deeper into himself.

His eyes rolled back into his head as he threw his head onto my shoulder. "Yes baby," I said, "you sound so delicious, give me more." I squeezed his sac with increasing pressure, and his cock continued to bounce strongly, surging full of blood. I returned to his cock and got a firm grip on his thick eight inches of uncut, dark meat. His member jolted in my hand, becoming stronger and firmer. I strengthened my grip and re-adjusted my fingers so I could cover as much of his cock as my hands could grasp, and I stroked him toward the first glistening of precum. And he moaned so beautifully, his eyes fluttered, and his head was back with his mouth open; and that rock hard penis in my hand while I was gripping with all my might made me wonder if he would faint. I centered my stance in my Doc Martens.

His body dropped into my arms, and I held him up with my left arm, supporting his body against mine. I coaxed him, "Yes baby you feel so good in my hand," while I stroked his cock, never loosening my grip, his rod throbbing in my hands, meixing the sweet pain with the arousal of his body calling out for more. We ached together, yearning for release.

We danced this dance for over two hours, me letting him breathe deeply, moving all the endorphins through his body. Then, when my grip on his balls or cock was causing his breathing to stop, I relaxed just enough to see the bobble of his penis ache for more. He was a wonder to behold, this combination of intense pain and the joy of a hard erection. His sounds were guttural and the intensity made my own primal nature rise. I once again returned to his balls, only this time to twist and squeeze and then, with both hands now taking their place, one on the cock and the other on the balls, it was time for the crescendo.

And what's in it for me, you ask? Giving intense pleasure. Bringing someone into that subspace without drugs is a powerful experience. I have enjoyed both sides and breathing the air of your submissive is like drinking in the endorphins that are also being shared. Power Exchange—it's my natural high.

Is CBT for You?

Don't ask me why some men like having their naughty bits punished with cock and ball torture, but they do. And my favorite bottoms are the ones that really, really do.

So picture the scene: I'm at my favorite dungeon on a Saturday night. In walks a 4B - Beautiful, Buff, Bald, and Black I call this the 4B's of Destiny, because he is, destined to play with Me. Then picture him naked. His brains, name or height don't matter, just enjoy him oiled up and blindfolded.

I check the time, this scene could last two hours and since I didn't get a nap before starting to play at 11:30 pm, two hours of intense poking, slapping, hitting, pumping, and twisting can wear me out. Then we must be in a space conducive to fluid spillage, arm and leg room to swing and kick, and seating and/or laying options. I like my bottoms to be as comfortable as possible for the pain I inflict.

Nerve endings are beautiful things. The more sensitive the skin area is, the more nerve bundles there are to play with. They register pain and pleasure faster and when syncopation occurs, the nerves can no longer distinguish pain from pleasure. Just watching the body writhing in reaction to the stimulus of slaps, strokes, or bites can bring the utmost delight.

Since I'm in the mood for stingy vs. thuddy pain tonight, I choose my instruments carefully. Knives are the first course to start my encounter with his skin. I trail the cool flat stainless steel blade slowly, watch the skin and fine hairs prickle in response. Then I dip the tip, creating pools of just enough pressure but not enough to pierce through the skin. Whether I use one blade or two, I create a symmetrical dance undulating across the smooth surface. I put on a pair of my Love Bites Vampire Gloves and lightly touch flesh. His skin is all goose bumps now, and I head to his throbbing cock. He's uncut and the extra sensitivity is just what will drive him crazy with craving and mad with the intense pleasure. I slowly wrap my hand around the head, pulling the foreskin. He jumps and then leans into the gloves' grip. He tosses his head back and forth, shaking it violently to clear the flood of chemicals in which he is now drowning. His body has signaled that I have him where I want him. Skin shudders as the nerve endings are sending both pleasure and pain messages to the brain.

A study from Radboud University Nijmegen in the Netherlands shows that men's cognitive performances were impaired when they were around women. I was shooting for maximum cognitive failure and the limpness of his arms, the surrendering of his cock to my use, made it clear he was mine to do with as I pleased.

It felt like I raced through the next hour and a half, teasing his flesh, making his body arch and moan. His pool of precum made a sticky mess everywhere. I knew he was aching to cum and each time the tip of a blade crossed the tip of his cock or my gloves gripped his cock hard and stroked, he would spurt a little more precum.

Now he was ready to be mounted. I instructed him to stand, his eyes barely coherent to my instructions, gave him water to drink, and then forced him to his knees facing my "bro" cock. He dined hungrily on it, moaning in pleasure and stroking his own cock.

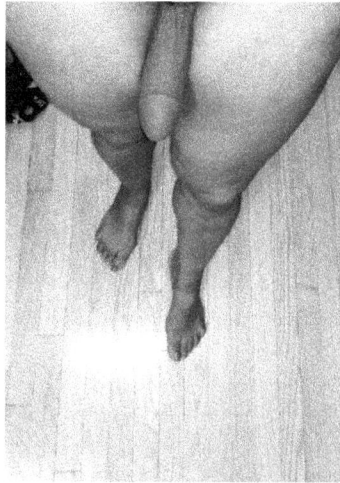

My BBC!

"No, no pet, all the cocks in this room are mine and for my pleasure and use," I said. He removed his hand, and I watched his cock strain for release. "Get me good and hard so I can take you like the bitch you are," I commanded. He eagerly sucked my silicone brown cock, sloppily reveling in the noise and his enthusiasm for what was next.

"Good boy, your reward is coming."

I had him bend over the massage table, my cock dripping with a mixture of precum and spit. I added more of my own spit and saw his rosebud already peeking open. "Pull back those cheeks, slut. I know you want this."

He moaned, reached back and pulled his ass cheeks apart.

"Yes Mistress, take me, make me your bitch."

"You are already are." And I slipped the head of my cock into him, and held it. He pushed back, eager for the whole thing inside him.

"Greedy little slut aren't you?" His hole was surrounding my cock quickly. I moved his hands and put mine on his hips, centered myself, feeling the ache of my inner cock wanting to devour him.

I slowly worked his ass, pumping and letting him feel like a well-loved bitch. While he was eagerly fucking me back, I put my vampire gloves back on.

"Are you getting close pet? You ready for me to let you cum?"

I reach around and grab his cock. He jumps and pushes back even harder on my cock, giving himself what his body craves. Stroking his cock, I put my thumb on top and let all four digits grip the underside of his cock. He shudders, stopping for a moment to catch his breathe.

"Yes Mistress take me, I'm yours, all yours."

I smile, thinking, *tell me something I don't know*, and start timing my strokes in unison. It's time to build up the rhythm of threes and sevens. I fuck and jack his cock off so hard that when he comes he arches his back and shoots out across and over the massage table.

He's a limp doll afterwards. I pull out of him, release him to recline on the table.

"Don't think you're done, slut." I remove my dildo and motion him to crawl to where I'm now sitting, spread-eagled and dripping.

"Serve me."

Make Me Submit!

If I had a nickel for every time a guy says that to me, I'd have a bag of useless nickels. Really? I have to make you submit? Like I have to make you clean your room, or pick up after yourself? That never works. So don't expect it to work in your kink life either.

Only thing I will force you to do is be honest about:

Your pain threshold—Bucking up and taking it is plain stupid.

Your marital status—The loneliest men are married to good women.

Your experience level—Very dangerous for you to get into a scene where you don't fully understand how it will play out on your body.

Your health status—Don't spread your germs please; there are always safe ways to play.

Your mental health—Very dangerous for you if some bad memory is triggered, and I can't help you if I don't know you need the help.

Your expectations—Guys, we know that deep down, you want to get off for free. We all do, but it doesn't work that way for long. Admit it and then be prepared to negotiate what you are going to give. Make it worth my time. Since girls are not like boys, quid pro quo on oral service skills probably won't cut it.

We'll get along much better, I promise.

Male Sluts: Not Just a Sport, But an Adventure

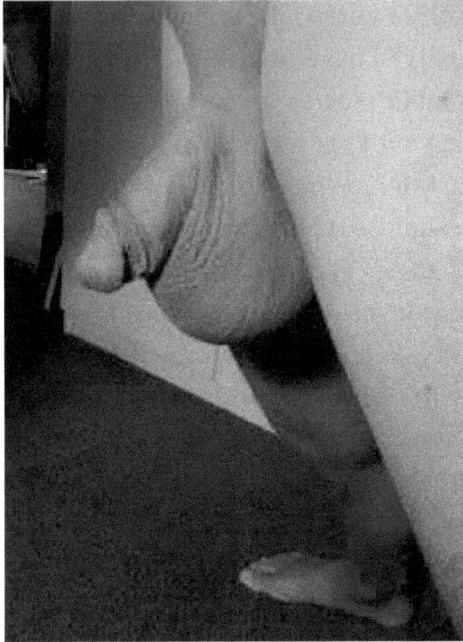

Swagger Power - 500ml of Saline

Okay I must admit that any time I can fill a man's ass or balls, I get wet— really wet. My hips get to gyrating, and I swear, I can't wait to come back again as a man and fuck something hard with what I hope will be the biggest schlong on the planet! Well, maybe not the biggest, because I hope I remember that as a female I was happiest with girth, not length.

So one weekend a male slut winked at me, saying those words I love to hear, which could be any combination of things like:

"Ooh I love the size of those hands, I wonder what they will feel like inside?"

"I love needles, you sure you brought enough?"

"Staple guns, hopefully you brought the 3/4" staples, they're my favorite!"

"Blow darts, that's been one of my fantasies!"

Nothing says *flirt* like those kinds of original lines and really, I never get tired of hearing even the bad ones.

So imagine my happiness when I started the evening with a request for canes and then got a lovely surprise with a request for saline and fisting, I was in heaven! Could I get it all done? It was after all a private play party, so I knew I had to move quickly. I started with the saline injections and continued to socialize, really wanting to leave my bottom, so I could jump right into caning; but, I recalled that recently when a distracted Domme friend took her eye off her bottom, he fainted and was injured. So I stayed put, but an hour later, and 500 cc's later, the swagger factor happened and I got my canes out. Happiness is multi-play scene nights.

Pound of Flesh:

Lessons in Sexual Objectification

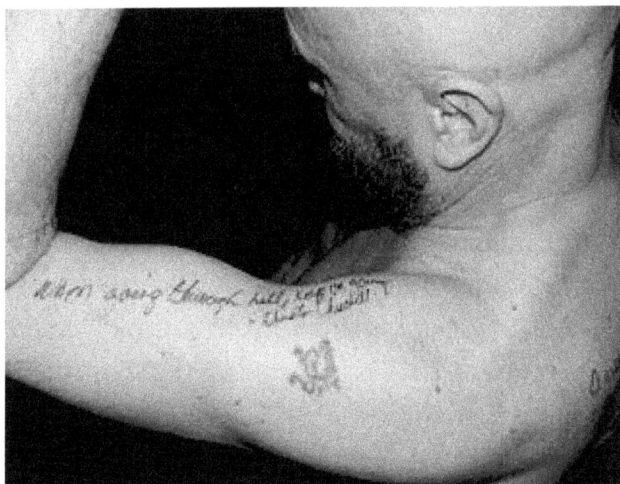

Gé - My Kinky Canvas

Growth itself contains the germ of happiness.-Pearl S. Buck

Gé suggested we use a smaller tip marker for our second night of play together in the dungeon.

It had been eighteen months since our last scene together. Then, I had gathered eight other women who took turns playing on two men hog-tied, laid facing each other and forced to suck each other off, while the women unleashed their unique sadistic natures upon their backsides. The play was impactful, gathering a tribe of women to exercise their primal urges.

But this year was different, the women each had gone their own way, and I wanted to orchestrate my own artistic drama.

"You know I like to bring you the markers for the writing." Gé was quick to remind me that he enjoyed the verbal humiliation play of temporary ink. His soft French accent made his words hang in the air in front of you, so you could see their richness. "There is a Japanese movie where I saw this couple. She used her male partner's body as a canvas and then in Japanese wrote erotic poems on his back. It was so sensual and so beautiful."

"I want to see that movie," I said. Gé was smiling. I thought the temporary erotic literary release was not only a beautiful image, but also a doable scene. His 6'2" canvas and shaven head sported a red, squared beard. His soft round head was a contrast to the angular lines of his chin, like a round ball sitting neatly on a square peg.

When we arrived at the dungeon space, we broke away to greet old friends before the evening play. I chatted about the new challenges of living out and the opportunities to celebrate that were now appearing daily. I joked with friends, "I should have come out when I was twenty, when my tits were still perky." I laughed at myself over the wasted years of chasing lesser pleasures.

"Madame Serene," Gé crooned in my ear standing behind me, close enough to share his warmth, though the night had already dropped to 55 degrees and he was naked except for his boots.

A hard man is good to find.-Mae West

"Come Gé let us begin our literary odyssey. I see my muse has a rise." I felt his hard cock pressed up against the back of my thigh.

A man in the house is worth two in the street. - Mae West

I made a comfortable easel bed for my canvas to recline. Gé laid down on his back and smiled, waiting for direction. "Do you want to know what I write or will you look at it later?"

"It's good for me to wait for later." He closed his eyes and relaxed into the moment.

"Okay, be comfortable then, sleep if you want to, no need to help me. I want to let the markers and the words find their places on your body."

I began listing my favorite quotes, which for the evening resonated with at least two of my lower chakras:

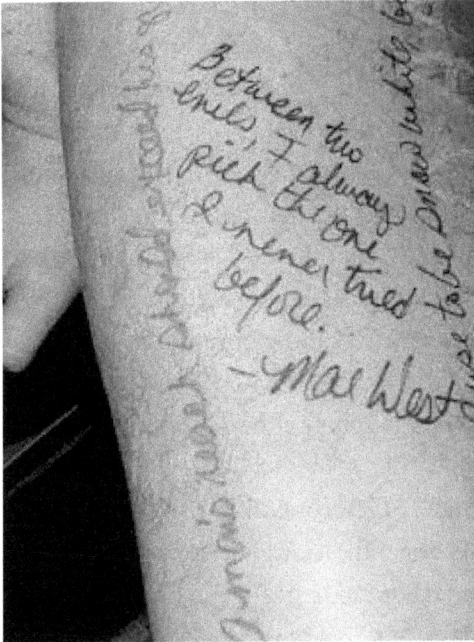

Gé - My Kinky Canvas

In order to know virtue, we must first acquaint ourselves with vice. - Marquis de Sade

A dame that knows the ropes isn't likely to get tied up. -Mae West

Anything worth doing is worth doing slowly. -Mae West

I praise loudly. I blame softly. -Catherine the Great

The authors, all my heroes, set forth words that were breadcrumbs to my soul, reflections and wisdom beautifully captured like little ghosts of truth.

The music from the main room drifted softly, buffered along by the sounds of laughter by the fire pit and a woman releasing wails in bitter moans that penetrated to the bone.

Sex is emotion in motion. -Mae West

Colors chose my hand and with the rise and fall of his chest, they called for the words.

I speak two languages, Body and English. -Mae West

The smell of his skin was a blend of artificial product and sweat. The slight salt of his skin tickled my tongue and left me with a craving for more.

A man's kiss is his signature. -Mae West

Heads popped into the room, left unlocked, but our scene carried its own air of intimacy and despite the space for more play, we were left alone.

Sex is a part of nature. I go along with nature. -Marilyn Monroe

I only like two kinds of men, domestic and imported. -Mae West

I straddled his chest, my pens gliding across his skin, not pinching, hurting, scratching, or biting. Words fell onto his flesh and their power resonated back into me. The words became flesh.

It is always by way of pain one arrives at pleasure. -Marquis de Sade

A body, whether it be male or female, brown, beige, ecru, or ebony, is alive and beckons.

I am a woman who enjoys herself very much; sometimes I lose, sometimes I win. -Mata Hari

Each word carried the possibility of love lost, taken, given, and forgotten.

Between two evils, I always pick the one I never tried before. -Mae West

Gé needed a smoke break, and I finished the front of his body, enjoying what I put onto flesh and made alive in my memory, my present frame of mind, and my desire to finish.

I like restraint, if it doesn't go too far. -Mae West

I only have 'yes' men around me. Who needs 'no' men? -Mae West

When we both returned from our breather, I moved Gé onto his stomach and began to feel a need to display the rules—

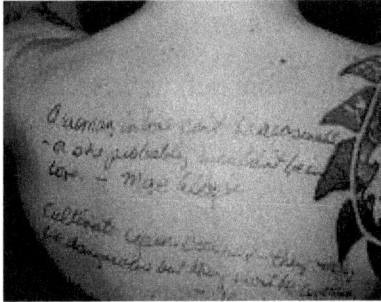

Gé - My Kinky Canvas

I may be kindly, I am ordinarily gentle, but in my line of business I am obliged to will terribly what I will at all. -Catherine the Great

Catherine always sobers my mind and forces the harder edge up to the surface. She, a woman of forced destiny, who took her pleasure and owned her world. She speaks to my desire for power.

History will be kind to me, because I intend to write it. - Winston Churchill

I once again straddled Gé and moved over his left leg. One spot in particular, his left heel, was perfect for stroking and hitting my clit.

The question isn't who is going to let me; it's who is going to stop me. -Ayn Rand

The room began to fill with other scenes, joyful and sexual and welcomed to share the top/sub space created.

I used to be Snow White, but I drifted. -Mae West

I lifted and slipped my now engorged clit over the heel of his boot. And began to write:

The idea of God is the sole wrong...

I dropped my head onto his relaxed buttock. I wanted to smell his flesh connecting my words, imparting my will if ever so lightly pressed on. I was enjoying riding his boot, while he lay perfectly still—object and palette.

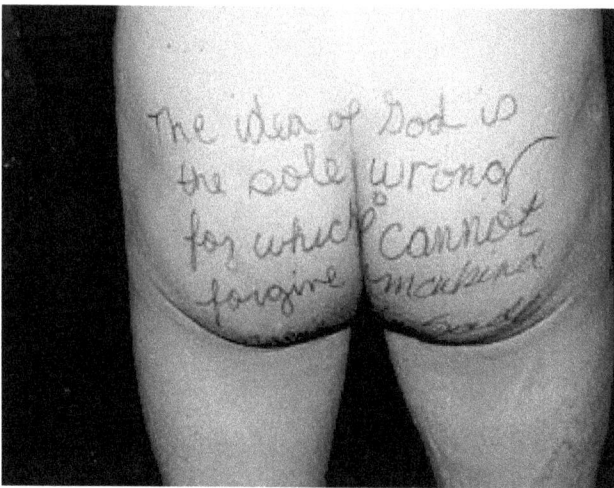

Gé - My Kinky Canvas

...for which I cannot forgive mankind. -Marquis de Sade

59

I only grunted to hear and confirm my own pleasure. My orgasms are my priority and I take them as I need them, no matter the place, the body, or the frame of mind.

Satisfied, I laid down next to Gé and was happily ready for a traditional smoke. My giddiness seemed a bit out of place as I felt like a school girl ready to show off my new art. And, this recess experience of play made me feel twelve again.

The Edges of Pleasure

Travelogue from DESIRE

Leather Women Unleashed, June 2008

DESIRE is a weekend long retreat held in Palm Springs every June. Leather Women from around the world gather to get what I call their PhD's in debauchery. The mecca for kink skills learning and the ripest lowest hanging fruit of beautiful women all ready to play with you.

-

My First DESIRE: It was really hot, so clothes were the first things to go. DESIRE is hosted annually at a resort in a beautiful development of small resorts catering to gay (really buff) men. We were the talk of the neighborhood, and each time I stepped outside our private courtyard to retrieve something from my car, I was stopped by a curious man inquiring about the women they were seeing and what sorts of debauchery were going on in there. The entryways to these resorts are typically open to men who cruise in and out, but ours was closed, and they kept hearing and wondering about the many moans, shrieks, and laughter pouring over our walls day and night.

At just over a hundred womyn in attendance, 10% were Women of Color (WOC), representing Leather women from Vancouver to San Diego. The event is part workshop, part play party, and part networking event, and gives women of all sizes, identification, and preferences the freedom to look openly, strip easily, ask questions, participate, and snuggle up to a voluptuous pair of breasts.

Friday night opened with a dramatic Japanese style drumming by a professional musician and martial artist. She is a "bratty bottom" of Japanese descent who, while drumming, was also being caned. The performance was intense and beautiful. She also taught an excellent workshop on Impact Play, which taught practical ways to hit with increased accuracy and power with minimal effort and reduced risk of injury.

Saturday and Sunday workshops ranged from anal and dildo play to three different workshops on blood play, advanced bondage techniques, playing with brats, fire play, Florentine flogging, and underwater bondage complete with scuba gear! I recognized some of the presenters from HBO's "Real Sex." On average, each had fifteen-plus years of experience in the kink lifestyle.

But Saturday night was one for the record books. "Fista-thon" was an open competition to beat a record of thirty fists in forty-five minutes. Three lovely fistee holes entered the competition and, though not a novice, I earned a new red hanky for my personal best of three vaginas in three minutes. The winner, with a whopping fifty-three fists in forty-five minutes, upset the former "Title-holer."

The event was not without its intimate and intellectual stimulus as well. On-site was a sex researcher, recording stories and experiences about the non-normative sexualities of women. This is important research for the next Kinsey report for the coming generation of women in kink.

Later Saturday night, the fire play women came together to share fire eating, dancing, and even flogging techniques. The night lit up when willing victims were covered in alcohol and set on fire and then jumped into the pool; it was colorful, hilarious and astounding.

There was plenty of time to lounge around the pool, get to know womyn, bois, former girls now boys, former boys now girls, and all ranges in between.

I met a beautiful sister Top from Vancouver. She shared the same lament about few WOCs who would come out to events in Canada. Then it hit me, our people are still in the closet. We can learn from the GLBT community who have gone before us, opened the world to acceptance and even marriage in many states. Living in one of the most liberal states in the Union, I realize it's our turn to open the doors for ourselves, each other, and our younger brothers and sisters to follow. To quote Mahatma Gandhi:

"First they ignore you, then they laugh at you, then they fight you, then you win."

DESIRE weekend was a slice of heaven, because it was acceptance. I encourage you to find that place "out" among your friends in kink.

School Time

My 2nd DESIRE

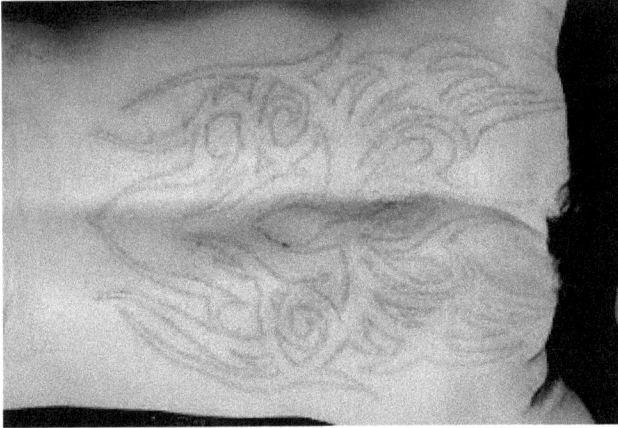

Courtesy of PhoenixB, Seattle

DESIRE is all about upping your game with women you respect, admire, and want to play with. When I met Phoenix from Seattle, I knew I was in for a treat. Phoenix is one of the founders of Wycked Women in Seattle, and her Cree heritage brings a unique spirituality to her scenes. She's an artist with a scalpel and her work (pictured above) was a lovely treat for everyone.

But it was later in the evening when she pulled out her secret ingredient and brought a fire to dance on the skin like none I'd ever seen before. We called it the Secret Sauce. I got my hands on some as soon as I could. Can't wait to bring it home to the troops.

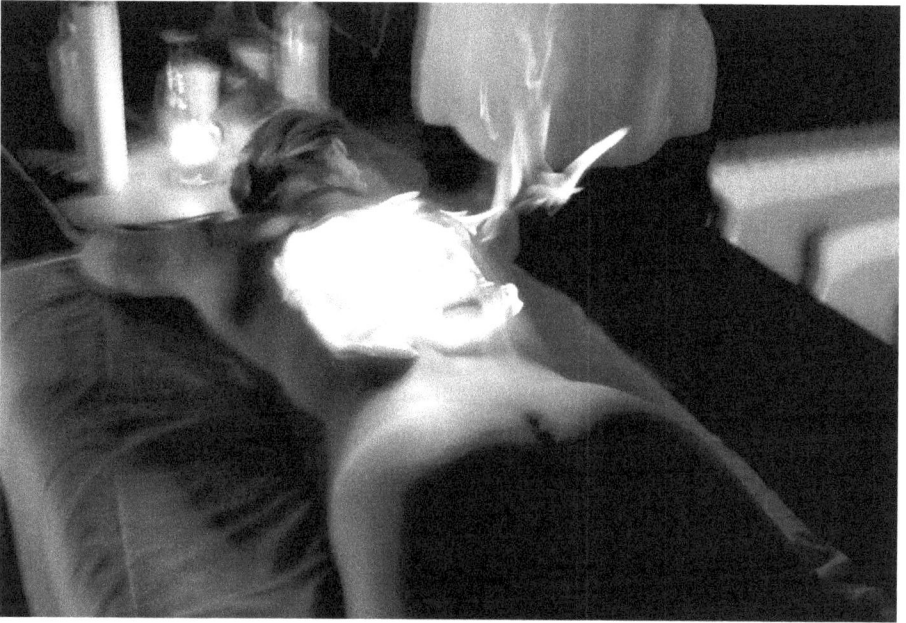

Courtesy of Katy TheShuggafree

Pilgrimage

It's that time of year when trickling sweat trails down between my breasts, rounds the cup of my cleavage, and begins to turn into passion. Juices signal and flow between my legs and the giddiness of junior high returns as I start to pack my good floggers and fire wands. Cue the drum-roll, it's DESIRE time—my third!

And it's been a fucking long year, and I can't wait to dip myself in the honey of women's pleasure that is the divine kinkland of the Palm Springs desert. This year, instead of running from one workshop to another, I am giving one of the workshops, teaching fire play and saline infusion. But I do hope I can get into the suturing and branding classes. I so enjoy learning and bringing more spice to my play.

With the struggle to survive in the vanilla world, this year's retreat is especially meaningful and it is rewarding to take a break from the "false world" and live my true kink self. How do we manage to keep it together, day in and day out … Smiling when we want to curse, biting our tongue when we want to tell it like it really is, and feigning embarrassment when sexuality comes into public view.

But I've accomplished one of my goals and am on my way to accomplishing more. I have challenged myself with the *what if* question. You know, *what if they find out? What if they know I'm kinky? What will they say or do?* So far I have found the answer is what "they" do is their business; what I do is mine. And I'm taking care of my business. And I may hurt someone, but only because they asked me so sweetly! MU-AAHHHHHHHHH

What Happens At DESIRE

Stays at DESIRE. We decided to adopt this motto that has caused smirks, winks, and nudges. In a resort full of low hanging fruit, women with the slightest breeze of suggestion are ready to play, and many of them are heavy with desire.

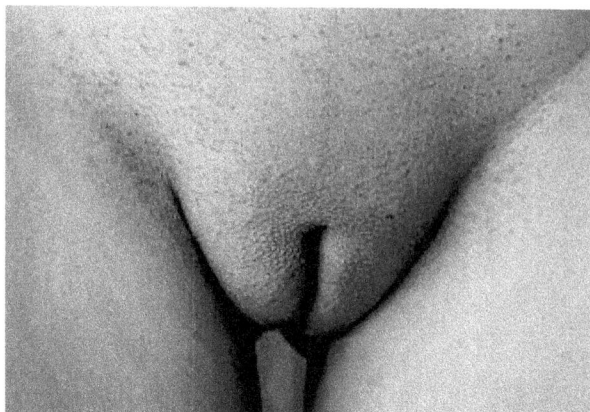

Theirs

I was satiated during my two-hour genitorture scene and expanded my concept of camel toe with a saline infusion that created a perfect one without the harness. And then I found new tricks and understanding of the extreme play of women that I previously failed to comprehend—or just didn't get.

I laughed, cried, danced, ran around naked, and snapped as many pictures as I could. Met some amazing women; one Domme offered her boi as stud service after she had sutured a dildo onto him for our use. A delightfully strong boi that came well equipped.

I wish I could share the pics with you friends, but let your imagination roll around to all the possibilities of space and time that can appeal to the horny woman who's interested. And then stand back and prepare to be amazed.

Women's Ways

This was sent to me by a vanilla friend, but it was too cute not to share:

Four friends spend weeks planning the perfect girls' getaway trip—shopping, casinos, massages, facials.

Two days before the group is to leave, Mary's husband puts his foot down and tells her she isn't going. Mary's friends are very upset that she can't go, but what can they do ....

So when the three get to the hotel only to find Mary sitting in the bar drinking a glass of wine they are quite surprised.

"Wow, how long you been here, and how did you talk your husband into letting you go?"

"Well, I've been here since last night. Yesterday evening I was sitting on the couch, and my husband came up behind me and put his hands over my eyes and said 'Guess who'?

"I pulled his hands off to find all he was wearing was his birthday suit. He took my hand and led me to our bedroom. The room was scented with perfume and filled with two dozen candles, and rose petals all over.

"On the bed, he had handcuffs and ropes! He told me to tie and cuff him to the bed, so I did.

"And then he said, 'Now, you can do whatever you want.'

"So here I am."

Fisting

I love fisting! Vaginal is nice but anal is much better, mainly because you can go deeper and provide more stimulation for both you and the bottom or submissive with whom you are playing.

I recently played with a femme who is a switch. She has a high pain tolerance and loves to be left with marks. So I put her up on a cage, with a foam layer on top. I had her on all fours, her rear facing me. I started with some light caning and then progressed to my plastic rod, which delivers blinding hot licks and wicked marks. She was loving it. She is a primal player who licks her lips and moans with pleasure as the intensity goes up.

I then moved to cupping. Cupping is an Asian medicinal treatment (you can find pictures on You Tube, I'm sure), which redirects blood flow just underneath the surface of the skin. I know that the cups are fun to apply on the body and become a great massage tool. But this was lightweight stuff for this girl. So we moved back to her rear end, and I put my rubber gloves on.

I should mention that three babies have flowed out of her body and has made the passage upward easier, and it's quite enjoyable for her to finally be filled up. Little lube was needed as she was already wet and dripping. I love the place when all four fingers are going in, and you are waiting for her body to relax and take the knuckle. Her vagina was hungry for filling, and she pushed back on my hand so it went in quite easily. Then the fun began.

Finding her uterine wall was like spelunking. You feel around for the walls and look for new ways to move about a cramped space, surprised how much of your body is now in hers. I crooked my index finger and began to stroke the wall that delicately separates her vaginal and anal canals. She moaned and smacked those lips. I kept stroking that spot, rolling my

70

knuckle all around, back and forth, till she came so hard she squeezed my wrist tightly inside.

Even my attempts to pull out made her come harder. But after a moment she released her grip, and I rolled around again to make sure we got all of that orgasm out., I slowly pulled my fist out and she hollered, "Oh yeah, there's the best one," with another fist gripping O.

When I released her, she collapsed down over the bed and let her orgasm energy swirl about our bodies. She got up, dressed, and said, "I'm satiated". Zipping up my play bag I thought, *My work is done here, time to find more womyn in need of medicinal satisfaction.*

You Need Orgasms

We are all born with functioning sexual organs designed to supply natural pleasure for the body. Some of us get lucky and get both sets, but that has its challenges as well. Discovery Channel aired a documentary on women's orgasms. The scientists put a woman in an MRI while she masturbated and watched her during orgasm light up over eighty sections of the brain, providing it with oxygen and nutrients. That means we feed the brain every time we orgasm. It makes perfect sense, since we are designed to procreate. We signal the body to stay healthy, useful, and regenerative, as orgasm is still needed for reproductive purposes.

An old wives tale goes like this: If you put a penny in a jar every time you make love during the first year of marriage, then take a penny out of that jar every time you make love for the rest of your marriage, there'll still be enough money left for the flowers at your funeral. We are designed to fuck. Our culture has controlled our procreation urges. We are taught to disapprove anything beyond those created rules. That's not healthy for us.

Our closest genealogical relative is the Bonobo monkey, and they fuck everything all the time and, guess what, they are the most peaceful creatures. We could learn something from our ancestors.

We are sensual beings, all desiring the positive elements of our senses: Food and drink with taste; pleasant floral, musky smells for our noses; art in whatever form of beauty the eyes perceive; music, rhythmic sounds, soft voice, lectures, poetry for the auditory; the written word for the auditory digital; and human touch and other kinesthetic experiences that give us physical pleasure.

Dacher Keltner, in his book *Born To Be Good*, teaches us the biological importance of emotional pleasure for the physical body. His understanding of the common emotions represented across all humans and mammals alike show the clear natural values we should give to pleasure. It is innate to our being ...

Followed finally by the erotic. This is a learned skill. Not developed until some level of maturity of the individual. Many of us don't reach it till our maternal and paternal duties are over with. The kids are gone, leaving the bored husband and wife looking at each other wondering, *Is this it?* The unfulfilled fantasies come back with a vengeance, and like a bad cold, they won't release you till they have left your body.

It's the way the body signals it's time for growth. Fantasy like dreams are a way the body communicates a need to you. Have you ever had a dream that keeps returning? Does it get louder each time, turning into a nightmare? Dream research teaches you that you are ignoring something when the dream gets louder. If, for instance, you are getting chased constantly in your dreams, then you are running from something. Dreams provide a metaphor to the emotional issues in your life.

Fantasy represents emotional hunger. It allows our bodies to come into the yin-yang balance of our natures. We desire and fantasize about emotional states of pleasure we would like to be in. The most common in the kink community, because of the size of the population, is the heterosexual male's desire to be in submission, laying down the burden of making all the decisions.

I have often thought that women of my generation have been afforded the luxury of choice by taking the easier road. They cry, "Just tell me to do what I want to do." And you know what? I would have cried that plea too, but I like making decisions. As with gambling, I don't always win and the losses are sometimes painful, but I own them all. And that's why I'm a Domina that needs an occasional switch opportunity to rest my weary head upon. I'm the better for having loved and loss.

Both sexes in all cultures have a ways to go in learning how to be comfortable in our alignments. The Northern European cultures, which threw out the hard liner religious views and have adopted open sexuality and drug use, still boast the lowest crime rates. You would think we could learn from that. Our dogmatic religious beliefs have atrophied the brain[3]. And we simply get stuck in stupid.

Orgasm Recipe for the Busy Woman

Prep Time: 12 years
Cook Time: 5-10 minutes

-

List of Ingredients:

Clitoris - It may not have worked in some time, but as long as it functioned once, or came close to functioning, you're good to go. Clitorises are like old cars. A good priming of the pump will bring up that motor of pleasure and healthy living, getting you back on the road of life.

Stimulation device - For the purist and religious types I recommend going natural with fingers. For a quicker, *let's get her done* style instrument, I recommend a battery operated vibrator; however, knowing the carbon footprint of this device may unnecessarily ruin your orgasm process. Using electrical implements already in the house, such as a hand mixer with out the beaters or the corner of the washing machine, may be better.

Power Source - Please check battery strength on all vibrating materials. Dying batteries at the peak need of performance will result in a long, bitchy day to anyone in vocal range of you.

Lubrication - Nature again has provided our bodies with the best lubrication from two sources. Saliva is the best starter lubricant. Your vaginal juices once flowing are the second best lubricant.

Location - Beds are optimal, however, items like dirty laundry or an unmade bed can be orgasm-killing distractions. Search for locales that are inviting for orgasm escapades. If you enjoy the thoughts of feeling dirty or bad, the laundry room may be the perfect place, or the floor space in the living room or the guest bedroom may work. If you happen to have a marble kitchen counter, consider yourself lucky, and clear space enough for you and your big cool marble-hot flesh fantasy orgasm. Bathtubs are also excellent locations to recline, using the water spigot as a powerful and natural instrument of pleasure.

Music - Sound has always been a great relaxing aid for mood setting of any sexual practice. Quick and easy orgasms are not often completed in the length of one song. A note of caution: relaxing instrumental music may be used if the music does not cause a sleep reaction in your body. If you set up in riskier locations, your children may find you sprawled out on the couch with Yanni playing and your vibrator still buzzing. You may end up having an early discussion of family sexual practices at an inconvenient time.

Visual Memory/Fantasy - These are also an excellent stimulation aids. For illustrative purposes I will share with you an example I use frequently: Charlie from my graduate studies program. A young man still in his high sperm production age, Charlie is hot, though he constantly hides under a baseball cap, with dark frame glasses and way too much clothing. But upon closer inspection you discover thick black phallic eyebrows, smooth Arabian skin, and soft dark brown eyes with the obligatory long lashes. Stalking him for a significant time you will catch a glimpse of his thick, strong, head full of black hair—the kind of hair that's like a rein you pull while riding his hips in the Cowgirl position, achieving your galloping orgasm. But his best feature: his hands. He's a writer and has fine, white-collar hands. These are the kind of hands you imagine stroking your spine, pulling the hair on the top of your head just as you are at the point of your orgasm, or slapping your buttocks, evenly and consistently, in a manner that further stimulates your whole vaginal area. I recommend taking the time to visually undress him and concentrate on his erection beginning to rise through his clean white boy shorts. The contrast of his dark olive skin against those tight, white, mid-thigh length shorts are the only bow necessary for my X-mas Lexus parked out front.

Practice imagining his body, responding to you watching him reveal himself, solely for the purpose of your orgasm and visual pleasure. In your mind, turn his body around and watch him bend slightly as he removes his shorts. Your eyes then can feast at two perfect buttocks for stroking and gripping pleasure. I am personally working on a Charlie Pole Dancing routine, ending with Charlie swirling around, advancing down the pole, erect and dripping with pre-cum to my waiting, wet vulva.

Directions:

Prep the area if it has not been used in quite some time. Mix above ingredients in the order of priority of your body's response.

Begin stroking the spots that call for attention.

Continue stroking, adding visual stimuli as necessary. You should begin to feel flutters of pleasure starting to release in your lower body.

Add kegel exercises as necessary. This combination will guarantee reaching an orgasm but must be practiced. Flutters will continue as long as the body is coming closer to orgasm, however, forgetting to breathe will stop the flutters, but the kegeling, along with long oxygen pulls, will stimulate the wave producing orgasm expansion of this recipe.

Allow the body to continue its tremors with gentle stroking, applying just enough pressure to be interesting and not annoying. Let the "waves" of orgasm flow over the body until they subside.

The endorphin producing orgasm will allow your body to relax, rebuilding physical, emotional, and mental properties your body needs. Practice this orgasm-making recipe often for a fuller, richer, happier life. You cannot have too many orgasms in life. And for you religious types that had a stunted childhood, you are down tens of thousands. The good news is, the more you have the more you will want. And thanks to Charlie for so many lovely orgasms in his honor!

Option: For even quicker, stronger orgasms, remove all pubic hair!

Pain Is Your Friend

The philosopher Descartes hypothesized that pain and pleasure are part of a continuum. I like to think of it as a dance. The flow of energy from one body to the next is a beautiful mind fuck for me as a Dominant, and when done right, an amazing rush of endorphins for the sub, slave, or bottom sharing the dance.

Endorphins are the body's opiates, called up from exertion, stress, or pain, or for orgasms. That's the rhythm to the dance. Moving pain through a body to release endorphins is an art form for a Dominant or Body Craftsman. I can be as bold as to say it's what a good Dominant does. And that's what BDSM is all about!

Disagree? Philip Miller and Molly Devon wrote in the classic book on BDSM, *Screw the Roses, Give me the Thorns*, If the spanking is severe enough to warrant it, the brain signals the body to manufacture powerful, opium-like substances called endorphins, which enable people to endure high levels of pain. An endorphin rush feels great."

Remember when you had a loose tooth and you learned how to wiggle it to get just enough pain that you kept on doing it? That's endorphin rushing. See, you've been kinky for a long time.

Pain endorphins are not limited to a physical sensation, but they can be stimulated with humiliation or degradation play. Fear can bring endorphins to the surface and give you such a rush you'll feel giddy or drunk. Ask someone who likes horror films what they feel like. Ask an extreme athlete. They all chase the adrenaline and endorphins.

And pain players are my favorite. They see my serene smile the most.

Medical Kink

I'm ready to stretch and grow in a new direction this year. Medical play involves needle play, cutting, sounds, saline injections, enemas, examinations, and much more. At my doctor's nice sterile exam room, I'm always wet from the mix of anxiety that something could be wrong. I get weak in the knees feeling vulnerable and exposed in my paper gown. I lie back and let the aroma of my sex and anxiety rise in the room. I miss the days when you were alone with your Doctor and the sexual tension was thick. I liked seeing his head between my legs. Oh how I hate when the nurse comes in to join the examination.

My fantasy is to play Dr. Serene. I walk into a sterile room and get the strong whiff of sex and fear. Fear has a citrus smell, which mixed with sweat and the pungency of sex makes a powerful aphrodisiac. Fear and sex is best smell ever! (Be right back.)

(*12 minutes later.*) Where was I? Oh yes, examinations. Always important when about to stick, probe, or cut a piece of flesh. And oh, how I love the piercing of flesh. I love the living skin, how it responds to the rendering of itself, anxiously trying to regroup the cells and heal itself, yet bending and giving up easily to your sharp, persistent wrenching. The body is beautifully alive and to watch it work up close is geeky cool.

And I love the smell of blood, not the menstrual kind full of too much iron and dead cells, but the fresh sweet kind that is alive and full of oxygen. However, I do recall with glee fisting a young lady in the midst of her menstrual flow, which is incredibly therapeutic. Those cramped muscles hurt like hell and an internal massage is the best way to relieve the pain. I think of menstrual sex that way as well, medicinal, and when I screamed "Harder" for a reason. He knows I need a shot from his Dr. Feel Good.

So now where were we? Back to Dr. Serene, coming to a dungeon nearby soon. I make house calls.

Pin Cushions

Pin Cushions: love them or hate them, there is a frightening little rush from playing with this edgy style of kink. I'd watched enough of it over the years and, bored with my bag of tricks, I decided it was time to raise my skill level to include needle play.

For some reason I've seen more women than men drawn to this blood-letting sport. I'm guessing we women all used to the free flow of blood, so drawing it intentionally out of the body has its own peculiar enjoyment. A few weeks ago, the Los Angeles Radical and Wicked Women (LA-RAWW) had their first workshop at the beautiful Academy in downtown LA, and I made it a point to be there. The event was a pin cushion's dream, with a stellar lineup of Dommes: Olga, Mistress Shelly, and the host Domme introducing attendees to the sadistic, artful, and beginning elements of play piercings.

The demo models for the evening were a lovely array of self-described pin cushions. One young lady confessed to sticking herself not for the self-mutilating pain release like cutters do, but for the endorphin rush and high she received from this delicate and intense play. With each needle I placed into her she became giddier and flushed.

Over at Mistress Shelly's station another pin cushion was being adorned with butterflies, feathers, and beaded jewelry on suture thread. My discussion and learning included the use of a craft woman's favorite tool, the glue gun, for decorating needles with feathers to create those lovely angel wings I've seen on many FetLife portfolio pages.

Shelly's eyes began to gleam when a particularly handsome dyke bared her back for a little needle twisting that was getting the room turned on in the most primal way. There was barely a drop of blood in that scene.

Let me try to explain needle twisting: you insert the needle in a northward direction into and out of the skin, but before letting the stick rest you twist the needle 35-45 degrees to the east or west and insert it in and out again. If I explained it correctly, you should be thinking *ouucch!*

I left her only because "Ye Olde Violet Wand" was humming away at the medical station under Olga's delightfully intense hands. A lovely fair skinned lady with a couple of vertical rows of needles was being zapped with the wand, causing her to close her eyes and smile. Olga was then requested to pierce a mouth and nose bridge with a spinal tap needle. Her partner blu followed with a lovely sutured arm bondage. Visualize a row of needles on each lower arm, wrists up to the elbow. Then thread the needles like you were lacing your shoes. Then tie your shoelaces together, so that the arms are bound together. I'd like to see a bratty sub try to get out of that one!

I went home and bought my needle play kit that evening. I couldn't wait to get to the dungeon the following Saturday to find my own pin cushions to play with.

Kink Community

Six Steps to Sinning

Spend any time in the kink, fetish, or BDSM community, and you will find a lot of rules and protocols that at first do not make sense. These are there to protect you. We know learning the rules takes time and you will probably get your feelings bruised along the way. Don't worry about it; you and your partner should learn to get over it quickly.

I was asked once to give some quick tips on finding one's way into this world. Sure, the tips are quick, but they take some time to achieve. So here are:

My Six Not-So-Quick Steps to Learning Everything You Wanted to Know about Kink:

First step: Learn something. Go to a workshop, demonstration, class, or a meet and greet for kinky people. At least Google and seek one. Find out what educational opportunities are available at your local sex toy shop. Call and ask them to do BDSM classes if they don't have any. And then tell them to call me, I'll come and teach.

Second Step: Go to a Munch. This is a "meet and greet" of kink-curious people just like you, and it's held at a public restaurant or bar. Safe, easy, and you meet real people. Dress nicely, be your charming self, and look for like-minded friends and future play partners. They will probably not be your soul mate or the greatest Master of the universe, but they are never there when you're looking anyway. Plenty of nice, curious people do attend. Go meet them first with your clothes on.

Third Step: Go to a play party or a dungeon to just watch. Yes, you can go alone and not be noticed, touched, or hurt. Unless you want to play, that is, and then you need to ask someone. If you don't know anyone, just watch and listen. Whatever you do, don't touch anything or anybody without permission. Don't interrupt scenes by talking loud or asking questions of them while they are playing. Think of what you are viewing as a dance, you don't cut in.

Fourth Step: Self-identify your interests. Want to be spanked? You are a spankee, bottom, or submissive. Want to throw a whip or flogger? Then you are a Dom(me), Top, or Master. Want to experience both sides of the paddle? Then we call you a Switch. It takes time to learn your likes and dislikes, and you need to go through the first three steps to find out.

Fifth Step: Play with yourself or a friend, and don't play with a stranger unless you've completed the Fourth Step.

Sixth Step: Recover, make changes to your play list, identify your evolving self and desires, and then repeat steps 1-5. Keep playing and discovering. Repeat.

BDSM Church

My vanilla girlfriend of twenty years visited me this past week. After thinking about it for some time, I asked her if she would like to see my other life, the BDSM side. She thought about it for a moment, all the while I'm driving around in the neighborhood of the dungeon. I add we can pop in and see what it's like and take some of the mystery out of those dark places, I had only mentioned BDSM to her once ten years ago.

She says, "Sure I'm up for the darker side," and away we go. Upon entering we are both warmly greeted by a small group of my friends and after a tour, we sit around a lovely outside patio fireplace for more chitchat until someone decides to start playing. I brought no toys, so this was only a show and tell venture.

About a dozen people come in and say hello and at one point I asked my friend, quietly, how she was doing, and her response was, "This seems like church." I almost fell on the floor laughing and shared that with everyone around. Reverend Mel of Talking Sex Radio was there to share the pun and added, "Well, I am a Minister, so I guess so."

Who would of thunk it? My friends at the dungeon compared to churchgoers? So let me think about the similarities.

We meet to eat and drink before and after service.
We "belong" to this dungeon.
We respect each other's play.
We support new members with encouragement and answers to their questions.
We offer Saturday School for learning.
We attend conventions and seminars.

We dress appropriately for meetings there.
We practice privately and publicly.
We all believe we are called to this lifestyle.
We often suffer for those beliefs.
We can be persecuted for our beliefs.

I'll stop now before I begin to believe my own rhetoric, but first add that friendships are a precious gift worth working for, growing and stretching, and keeping for a lifetime. It doesn't matter how you've met, it matters what you've done after you've met. So be thankful for your friends, and tell them!

Our vanilla lives are sometimes bondages we cannot break. We who live in our own closets must bear our desires often privately, frustrated, berating ourselves for the natural desires within us.

For those of you out there, in that condition, come out and find friends and brethren of similar beliefs, practices, and kinks. There are safe places, there are people who will protect your privacy, and there is acceptance and fun awaiting you. Start with a simple Munch meeting, which is a gathering of kinky people for lunch or dinner. They are everywhere, and unless you are a public personality, you should be able to attend in your own community. If not, that's what conferences are for, and they happen all over the country.

And be grateful to be an American, where, unlike kinksters in other countries, pre- or extra marital sex won't get you arrested, jailed, hung, or stoned to death. We need to learn from the gay community, where ACT UP was formed, that we should not go out quietly. And when I self-identify kink as more than a hobby, as my self-identity, I will write about it.

BDSM Is the new Black!

One spring evening, Lady Pandora and I went to a vanilla club with a kink twist. The Boulet Brothers (though I only met one) hosted for the kink seeking vanillas "Miss Kitty's Parlour."

I was expecting a lot of "Stand and Modelers", but after the alcohol was flowing I found plenty of bottoms presenting themselves to us for our amusement. I thought, *What a lovely recruiting field for the community. Fresh meat!*

We in the world of kink after many years in the closet couldn't believe that what seems to us to be so open and out there is still a mystery to the general public. A hungry public. Well, that ought not to be!

I recall a Stockroom.com ad in the *LA Weekly* a few years ago:

BDSM is the New Black.

I thought to myself, *Hell yeah*! As us old timers are being clamored at to mentor and teach, it behooves us to remember that we are:

1. still sensitive creatures
2. breakable
3. easily embarrassed
4. have vanilla lives to protect at some level
5. in need of love and acceptance

There are a myriad of more things to consider, but primarily we are vanilla first, kinksters second.

Play safely People!

Wanted: More Sex Time!

Why didn't I run for a title in 1989 when I first heard about the possibility? I remember the younger Serene didn't need that pesky thing called sleep and got a lot more done in a day! Today my days are filled with charts, calculators, and many, many thoughts about sex, but very little time to act on it!

Shit, FUCK DAMN! When do I get mine?

Note: Women—My LIST is running off in my head like a machine gun!

Men—I'm too fucking busy, eat my pussy and go home!

Okay I'm better. I do miss the good old pre-AIDS days of zipless fucks. Now I can't find enough time to say *yes*. I didn't give out a lot of home numbers then or now. And the safety of a dungeon keeps the intimacy issues easily at bay. Say what? Yes, let me explain a common acronym in the kink community: CFNM—Clothed Female Nude Male. It's a classic role expressing the Female Dominance position in play, with the clothed person usually taking the Dominant position. I say usually, because one of the radical strengths of getting comfortable with your sexuality is dumping stereotypes. For example, Old Roman bath slaves were kept in some sheath while they did the work of bathing their Mistresses and Masters.

Like many of my peers, I am now missing the safety and intimacy of private play. I yearn for less chatting and more bare backing!

Public Disclaimer: I do not condone unsafe sex.

I just remember a time when all I worried about was the Clap.

I also know, I am damn lucky to have survived the 1980s, and my *Survivor's Guilt* is to help those who walk into the dungeons starving, with unfulfilled desires, and balance their way back to vanilla life of football, job, and family responsibility.

Do something different this year! Be your sexy self.

Now the Southern California Leather Woman *Work* Begins

I am reminded that it's time to put out for the 'community'. That was one of my campaign promises. Here's the results of my year as Southern California Leather Woman 2012. When it was my turn up to bat for the Leather Women's Community I managed two hits and a miss:

Three events:

Corset Fashion Show and afternoon tea an American style Tea with delightfully trained servants, imported teas, smoked poached egg finger sandwiches and delightful desserts, belly dancers, silent auction, decadent shopping and,of course, erotic art. We put on our best kinky day wear and raised funds for the Leather Archives & Museum, Women's Leather History Project. *The event sold out, raising the needed $700 to bring the Leather Women's History Project to Los Angeles.*

Education - Women's History Month was in March to celebrate the contributions of the Professional and Lifestyle Dominatrix , I played Kinky Oprah and hosted a Domina Panel. I'd come to know and admire several professional Dommes who have effectively managed their passions, careers, families, and vanilla and kink communities with grace and professionalism. They make me want to be a better woman, and I believe we can all learn something from their skills, stories, and histories. The Stockroom had graciously agreed to host the event and added a fashion show, drinks, food, music, and sales! *Even with torrential rains that day and the LA Marathon, we had standing room only and the best one day of sales for The Stockroom.*

Party - With my Sash Sistahs, let's kink it out DESIRE style. This event was for Radical and Wicked Women and smart men, a party to celebrate Sappho. She may have come from Lesbos, but don't forget she was bisexual. And so was the party, a meet and greet for the next Southern California Leather Woman.

Great beautiful event that was missed by its target audience. The theme of the party was based on the song "Pretty Girls Rock" by Keri Hilson, a song that, despite its first blush, is a celebration of the inner beauty in all women. I performed a pantomime to the song in drag as a man. The hatred of pretty girls is a sensitive topic that was just a bit too edgy for some of my sisters, and it is regrettable that this communication was lost.

Where Are All the Leather Women?

It seems with all the ease of *coming out kinky* these days that the traditional Leather Woman has somehow gone the way of the dinosaurs. However, when I look at the women in my community, I see smiling faces moaning with pleasure.

The landscape would look bleak with the absence of Leather Women in the bars. But what has transpired is an honest to goodness *paradigm shift*. The New Leather Women have moved to their own digs. They have formed clubs and created their own kinky self-expression. Whereas Leather Men may still socialize in a favorite bar, women have found different ways to meet their needs for kink expression.

"Kinky Women Who Like Kinky Women" is a Fetlife.com group for women that take their seduction strolls in social events and bathhouses, where they can be pampered and dip in and out of hot tubs and saunas, deliciously eyeing the selection before them.

The group description notes: The goal of this group is to create a supportive, friendly space where we can openly express our views, questions, and opinions on bisexuality, sexuality, gender issues, etc., and how they relate to BDSM or "What It Is We Do",[sic] understanding that we all do it differently and that that's ok.

It is a delicious feast to watch women in their mating dance. Women preening for each other is very hot. Clothed they may still look like your sister, mother, or neighbor, but when they come together they get stimulated and get off.

Los Angeles is a haven for the visual and performance artist. Watching New Leather Women at play is a creative delight—he creative flow of their kink as they decorate their bodies or their bottoms with feathered needles, paint, wax, or rope is intoxicating. I recall my friend Shelly com-

menting, "It's got to be pretty!" when referring to what gets her off sexually. Pin Cushion parties are well-lit affairs, where women gather to drink in
a room of endorphin rushing from the beautiful medical needle play.

Our groups are more diverse than ever before. We have found our
kink, and we gravitate to it. I won't get into the debate of which woman
has it best: the household slut who is pleased to get her pleasure from use
in a male Dominant household, or the Domina with a bevy of slaves eager
to be called to service her cunt, or the Master with her boi attending an AA
meeting.

The New Leather Woman is open to new experiences; she delights in
whatever kink or fetish makes her feel beautiful, hot, and horny. You'll
find the New Leather Woman taking up Belly Dancing, expressing her
sexuality with hips undulating as a siren call for pleasure.

Each woman has found a way to take care of her needs, as a Leather
Women should. Today she finds a myriad of choices. My Corset Tea Sa-
lon is for women who find pleasure in sensual dressing and being in beautiful surroundings. It is the *purposed sensuality* of beauty that makes me
wet.

The New Leather Woman can enjoy the decadence of an afternoon
high tea and shopping for erotic art; or the sensual drumming that comes
when women let their hair down at a Sensual Dance Party, where Belly,
Pole, Fire Poi, and Burlesque dancers entertain for seduction; and the
pride we find when we gather our intellectuals on Leather Women Panels
to celebrate who we are and how far we've come.

The title-holder role for women was birthed not out of a need to celebrate the bar patrons, but as an invitation to women to step up to the bar.
Duff Roberts, producer of the Southern California Leather Woman, has
charged her titleholders to "bring the women's community together" in
unique ways.

Domme Scouts have sprung up to fill a learning gap in the women's
community. Troop 96, (69 was taken by a group back east) Dominas come

to learn kink together by earning their badges and sashes. Submissives of both sexes are invited to take up learning as Brownies.

Female Domme Play Parties are the vision driving one Domina to gather women and men every Friday night of the month throughout Southern California. My friend, the Petite Princess of Pain, has organized thriving parties, so on Friday night you know a Fem Dom will be in charge somewhere in LA.

The professional Domina who takes the time to care for the married or closeted submissive has brought a tradition to the lifestyle that has not been lost on this observer. The Pro Domme takes her career seriously, continuously developing her professional skills, managing her family and her lifestyle play, existing as both the fantasy and memory maker on a daily basis. As Mistress Hikari of The Dominion says, "We are curbing anarchy and arrogance by offering a safe private means for licentiousness, while restraining impropriety, debauchery, and disorder." Thank a Pro Domme any time a judge, cop, or other male in authority goes easy on you. She has helped him maintain his balance in the vanilla world.

The promoters of our lives and history have not been forgotten. TSR Networks hosts three weekly shows, all by New Leather Women. Rev Mel hosts the original Monday night Internet show with a goal of "Changing the world one vanilla at a time." And community groups like LADs, Ms. San Diego Leather, and LAFEDS continue to nurture and welcome women into the lifestyle.

We have found ways of expressing our kinky lives beyond the leather bar or dungeon. Our lust for play is stronger than ever, and like water we will find our own level and take our own pleasure. Women still crave the company of those who get us and we will always seek our own way, eventually.

The Land of Enchanting Change

I keynoted at the 2010 Rio Grande Leather Conference. My speech:
Good Morning Gentle Kinksters:

Thank you, and yes I've come with my notes, reading glasses, and after last night, more gray pubic hairs *(groans & chuckles from audience.)*
What too soon? Ya'll wore a girl out, with all those hotties ya'll got running around here.

Greetings from Southern California. It's been quite an honor to be in
the Lland of Enchantment again this year, and thank you for inviting my
husband and I back.

What a weekend! Jason and Tyler, thank you. It always feels like a party with you two here. But you two MOFOs have fucked me over. It's your fault that I am sporting this new collar.

Ya'll I never talked to them, never knew their stories or struggles. I just saw them act all nice and normal and shit and I thought to myself they were nice people. And I wanted to be with them, to know them, to be a cool kids, like them.

IML 2010 Tyler McCormick, Master James, IMBB 2010-Jayson DaBoi

So after some soul searching I decided to run. After exposing my darkest fantasies, beliefs, and goals, all the other chicks quit and left me on stage, ALONE with the sash. And that's how I became Southern California Leather Woman 2010.

I've already learned from my sash sisters and brothers that this process is just another part of our evolution. For us, a public growth process, one for which I can't explain why, but know there is something we must go through, it's something, we are compelled to do. I have come to see titleholders as often our internal compasses, our politicians, preachers, reformers, and beauty queens, each in a unique way carrying OUR banners.

96

So this morning, after four hours of sleep from totally rewriting this presentation for the fifth time, I decided to talk about our evolution as leather people and gentle kinksters. With 300 million folks in this country, we here represent the hedonistic leaders of our country.

So what made us so fucking cool? I believe it's the evolution we have already experienced. Let me explain.

First the evolution of self:

How many had kinky thoughts or experiences before the age of sixteen? What about ten, five?

I believe we are here because you nurtured, or hid and protected, those thoughts, feelings, desires, and experiences until you found a safe place to express who you are. Once our sexual beings are awake we can not, or will not turn it off.

Second our play evolved:

From our cultural encyclopedia, *Screw the Roses, Give me the Thorns*, the authors write about the first time one of the authors lost a tooth. The pain was so good that when the second tooth starting coming loose he knew just how to wiggle it and make it hurt just right.

For me it was first grade with the towheaded little boy who would wait till I got on the swing sets and then start throwing dirt clouds at my ass. Humph, talk about a motivator. I swung higher and longer than the big kids.

My Dad's *Playboy*, *Penthouse*, and *Hustler* collection fed my masturbatory needs. Masters and Johnson taught me about my orgasms, and then I worked to perfect them.

Thirdly - That led me to evolve my relationships.

My first sexual lover was thanks to the Girl Scouts. Circle jerks were more of a lateral, share the twin bed in the dark, routine. But it sure was effective.

Next came the messiness of boys. I wanted to fuck boys purely on the basis of science. Didn't you?

I remember lying there not impressed with the particular motion of the ocean, if you know what I mean? But I was quite interested in scooping some of the white glue stuff and putting it under a microscope to see if I could see the little critters trying to crawl into me. They were alive and coming after me, like some kind of Amazonian killer ants. I was *scurrred ya'll*. But I was still horny.

When the pill came in the 1970s, that began our era of sexual play. I know I took lovers and shed them like used Kleenex. But I got mine, ya'll.

But after about a fifty or seventy-five, okay one-hundred, I got bored, and I wanted more than the swimming masses of dying sperm inside of me. I didn't want my pussy to be a dead zone. I wanted a brain and a heart to go with all the fun. Instead, I got distracted with a trip to fundamentalist land, with a charismatic Christian conversion, twelve years of celibacy, four years as a missionary, and two engagements. I knew I couldn't make that last commitment without trying out the merchandise. My thoughts were why put up with the bull, the sperm is always free.

I had to try out the boys before I would make a commitment. What I've learned about religious people is their brain atrophies, but first their dicks do, so I didn't marry them.

Next, I sought an evolution of Identity.

Along with the labels of race and religion, I learned about sexual preference. I was struggling with being a black woman in this country, making the lowest wages per capita and being told I had to work twice as hard to be given half the chance. That's when I noticed the GLBT community proclaim a self-identity and not just accept the labels dumped upon them.

The media helped. Some of you may remember in 1973 when Mark Segal, a Gay Liberation Front activist, interrupted the CBS evening news with Walter Cronkite. Because of that one brilliant act, the majority of Americans learned that there were gays in America.

Finally, that leads me to thinking about the Evolution of our community.

Unfortunately the Het Kinksters haven't had our Mark Segal moment. And the Internet for most of us has been our source for kink information.

We need our Stonewall. If a dungeon gets closed, many of us can hide our toys and go back underground. Unless the spotlight is on us, many of us cannot risk, and for so many reasons can't afford, moving into that spotlight.

But there are evolutionary steps we all can take. Organizations like the National Coalition for Sexual Freedom (NCSF) and the Woodhull Freedom Foundation lobby for and work to protect and educate our leaders so we don't lose our children, our jobs, or our security.

Tomorrow, after we come off our kink high for the weekend, we can take steps to move us further down our evolutionary path and as Americans practice our rights to "the pursuit of happiness."

Gentle Kinkster, I ask you to write one more check. Or better yet, go online and support the NCSF or Woodhull. Invest in ourselves, our community, our past, present, and future.

SLUT WALK - Los Angeles

What's wrong with Canada? The land of working socialized medicine took a step back in time when a Toronto Police Office told women to stop dressing like sluts so they didn't get raped. The Women of Toronto responded with, "Don't blame the victim." and Slut Walk was created.

On June 4, 2011, the Slut Walk Los Angeles rally and march was designed to bring attention to the female blaming patterns of the media and general public. The walk was a call to end rape and victim blaming—and to reclaim the word "slut." I marched. I hope you brought your slutty butt out and marched with me!

Hollaback is an international movement to end street harassment. We believe that everyone has the right to feel safe, confident, and sexy when they walk down the street. When street harassment happens, don't ignore it. Or forget it. Don't just walk on … Hollaback!

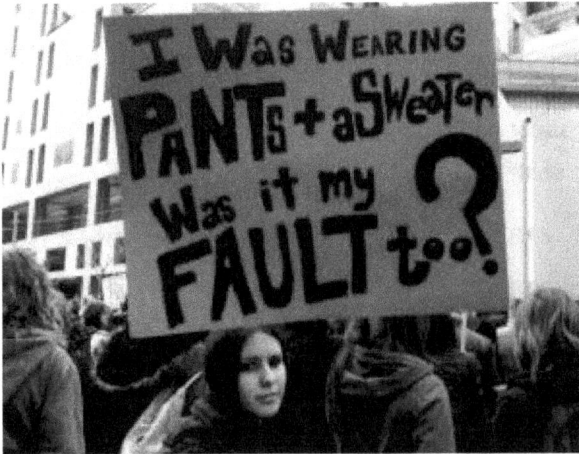

Follow them on Facebook: http://www.facebook.com/laslutwalk

Taxes

Its 2009 and I'm still in denial of the check I have to write to the IRS in ten hours, so I thought I would write instead. I've noticed that BDSM is getting more mainstreamed. Just recently this post appeared in a Fox News article: "To Be a Dominatrix." Sex expert Dr. Fulbright talks about the real physical labor, counseling, and earnings that young attractive females can make as a dominatrix. However, their earnings are substantially lower than high-end call girls.

Dr. Fulbright missed the point, I believe, in what draws most BDS-Mers to the professional kink world. It's not the money; it's the sheer joy of making a grown man cry, shout, cringe, sweat, and beg for more. It gets both of you off! We are the dirty deviants because we like playing with our whips and canes, and we spend a hell of a lot of money to obtain them. Then we are branded "Toy Pigs" when our shop-a-holic gene kicks in. We can't help it. We love the idea of their pain and our pleasure, maybe with a little humiliation and exhibitionism thrown in.

It's the same for the Lifestyle Dominant who spends considerable moola on toys, equipment and clothing in order to learn the BDSM arts.

Does that feel wrong to you and yet still tantalizing? If you are raised on sex is negative beliefs then you will find even more dark pleasure in the BDSM arts. It's the contrast of being bad that feels so good. It's part of our cool and kinky wiring. And please don't act surprised when you find a member of the kinky community right there in the pew next to you on Sunday.

Can you think of better way to spend a Saturday night than watching various beautiful naked women and men, standing in a darkened room, displaying their sex. Whatever instrument the Dominant chooses to use will bring the players to their chosen state, be it tears or ecstasy.

And who's paying? The Dominant most likely. Most BDSM players are at home in front of their computer screens instead of learning the finer details of specific and dangerous play. That's where the danger lies. Viewing online play and trying to do this at home will cause one to miss the warnings and danger issues that are not given on most sites. Who reads them anyway? I cringe when I see someone doing fire play on a website.

Kink is not just for the elite, but also for the illiterate. When dumb and danger mix, we have to call 911.

Be careful with your acts, words and your viewing habits. You can't write a check and make an accident oops go away. Play safe, sane, and consensual.

Californians: Time to Take Action

Our BDSM communities could be adversely impacted by a well-intentioned, but overly broad, piece of proposed criminal legislation that has been introduced by Senator Christine Kehoe (D) in the California Senate and set to become law as of January 2012.

SB 430 permits prosecution of strangulation or suffocation "in domestic violence, sexual assault, child abuse and elder abuse cases." But the bill's application goes far beyond those situations and results in felony prosecutions for use of hoods, gags and the like in BDSM play. There would be no requirement of intent to kill or injure," or of "visible injuries," and there is no mention of consent as a defense.

National Coalition of Sexual Freedom (NCSF) had proposed modifications of the bill's language that would address our concerns. They were ignored. So what's a kinkster to do? Be very careful with the use of toys in the mouth, your bottom could choke and you have a big "oops" that could cost you thousands in finds and up to six years in jail.

Update: SB430 passed and in January, 2012 became law. Leave your ball gag at home.

A Kink Is a Kink

I've chatted up a few of my Pro Domme friends just to see how they have managed their emotional, physical, and mental health with their work. Each lady had great advice to share. What is interesting to me, looking at the business side of this, is the need for the facade of bitchiness. I can't say I care for it and know I'll still be the "Laughing Domme" when I play because I think it's all very cool stuff.

I love the trepidation of players that are coming out for the first time. For them I feel like their drug pusher saying, "Come, my little slut and take a taste of the wild side. I promise you will be back for more." For others who just need an occasional fix, it's like enjoying a drink and smoke with an old work friend.

I'm an edge player, and I can still chart my course as I see fit. Laughing all the way! Define your kink as your choice and interest. We all get in trouble if we judge yours as bad and mine as good. No, I'm not going to find two examples in either direction to point to as standards for us all to follow. I have my standards; have your own. Build your own character and don't copy mine. Understand your kink is yours; someone will have a negative judgment on it. Adjust or ignore accordingly.

What a Wall Street Week!

When Wall Street imploded, the news caused me to wonder again about financial security nationally, locally, and personally. The news stories left me with so many reactions, such as:

-I felt my belly flop with the news of my bank going under.

-I saw red when I learned about the $700 billion dollar debt my government wanted to give away to bad bankers.

-I cringed with another arrest of a child sex molester, this time a preacher.

-I cursed when I saw that traitor Manny Ramirez clinch the NL West spot for the Dodgers

-I'm still holding my breath AL East spot for the Red Sox!

But I got wet when I read:

"Mistress Serene pounded my ass unmercifully and roughly, slamming the dildo all the way in and roughly back out again. In and out, in and out, while my ass got sorer and sorer. I cried out at each stroke. After a time she stopped for a rest. She sat down beside me where I could see her and that great big dildo. As she rested, she toyed with my dick, bringing it quickly back to life. She teased until I started dripping precum again and then stopped. The frustration of the teasing was starting to get to me..."

This excerpt is from a lovely tale of sadistic play written by a submissive male. I've had the joy of inflicting some erotic pain to his well-defined muscular body. It's a hot, action packed story he wrote for me when he was in particularly a high stress mode. He was a 1%-er.

I Love Japan!

I'm like a moth drawn to the flame when I watch the devastation that Japan faced with my childhood memories of living in that part of the world with the wooden houses. I could never understand how they survived the weather, let alone the devastation of a wall of water.

The earth is shifting whether we are ready for it or not. We can manifest the fear, the guilt for not doing something we should; we can plan for the "what ifs,", we can blame, or we can pray for the best. The story about the man searching for his wife continues to haunt me. I'm left wondering when ALL is washed away, who and what are we? What choices do we make going forward?

Shortly after I married, I learned a valuable lesson upon working in a small, disorganized crisis situation. As we were both Dominants, we were able to step in and take charge of the situations that needed order restored. It is comforting to know you can keep your wits about you when others panic and confusion rules the day.

For my own life, choosing to live as out and as honestly as I can, I thought I had reached the ultimate of living life fully. But when ALL is stripped away from you but your own life and the clothes on your back, your lifestyle choices still come down to being with those loved ones with whom you shared your life.

I keep asking what would I do when faced with this level of destruction? Am I prepared, can I survive? Can I pull it together, and rescue my own kin and neighbor? I expect that of myself. All the Girl Scout training and what I learned from my Dad is rote by now and it kicks in when necessary.

In the meantime, I'll go check my earthquake kits and make sure they are up to date. I will leave you with the reminder of the seven Ps: Proper Previous Planning Prevents Piss Poor Performance.

What Really Matters
Is What We Need

Our local kink community was reeling from the loss of three Leathermen recently. I only had a casual acquaintance with these men, but the impact of multiple deaths in a short time reminded me of an earlier time when Leathermen were being mourned from the AIDS epidemic—another period of loss that many of us only read about or remember from news stories of public mourning.

These unrelated deaths still tie us together with the remembrance that life is indeed fragile and temporary. We cannot expect to keep our looks, health, wealth, friendships, or our reputations forever. Though all of these attributes often weigh heavily in our lives and focus, when a loss of any of them occurs, all I really want is a hug.

A hug when given or received connects us skin-to-skin, heartbeat-to-heartbeat, breath-to-breath, and emotion to energy and power. All these areas we as kinksters delight in exploring, expanding, and reveling in; and we feel the loss of them when they are not available. Our hugs are the period after play, the welcoming for more play, and the invitation for intimacy.

I am grateful I have hugs in my life on a daily basis. You can have them, too. Hug someone you love, like, or want to know better; hug someone who needs it; or hug to share or receive good energy. Hug just because it feels good. It's what we need.

The WOODY AWARDS

Introducing the "The Woody Awards" by Me! These awards go to hot men, women, and inanimate objects that get my juices flowing, and make my internal penis stiff.

History of the Award: It began a few days after New Year's 2012, I was speaking out loud to the Universe while having a masturbatory flashback (MF) of the actor Kim Coates from Sons of Anarchy.

There was this scene where Katey Sagal caught him in the hallway before he was about to do the nasty with the housekeeper. But because he was "that nice kind of biker all girls want to fuck" he was considerate enough to run to the bathroom in her bathrobe for some baby oil. He's classic American Bad Boy, and that's why I love the writers of this show. Coates and Sagal imply in their shared MF moment (note the smiles) that he was so well hung, he needed to lube up.

I love remembering those moments with my own bad boys, and Coates has slipped in every time I put on my silk bathrobe. I also said to the Universe, "Next time I see him, I'm going tell him how much I enjoy him in my MFs."

Two weeks later, I'm at the LA Art Show sipping my first glass of wine and there is Coates with his wife and twenty-two year old daughter.

Now I've gone and run into him before I had a chance to think about what I would say. And all I worried about was how am I going to bring up the subject of Big White Cock (BWC) sex with his wife and daughter there? I couldn't go back on my word with the Universe and bring holy karma havoc on my head. So I politely chatted up the wife and daughter, both accomplished women in their own right, and then turned again to Coates.

"I must tell you I made a commitment to myself that when I saw you, I would tell you that how much I enjoyed the scene with you and the pink robe, however, I did not want to embarrass you in front of your family more than I already am at the present for just thinking about it." And I *serenely* smiled.

"Oh no, she's grown, tell me more." He smiled back, three inches from my own internal woody and then there it was, I sensed movement. My task was done. I delivered the woody. It was the least I could do for a scene well done. Congratulations Kim Coates for the First 2012 Woody Award!

Lesson: When you send a specific positive statement for the universe, be prepared for it to be answered.

Learning Something New

By Tuesday the Oxytocin Withdrawals Started Kicking in

A psychologist told me once that you have high oxytocin levels in your body after you have made love to someone for two weeks. So if you need to dump someone, stay away from that person until you are back in your own head, not craving their touch or kiss as much. Or as the elders would say, "Time will tell." But look at that ass, and tell me honestly: could you wait?

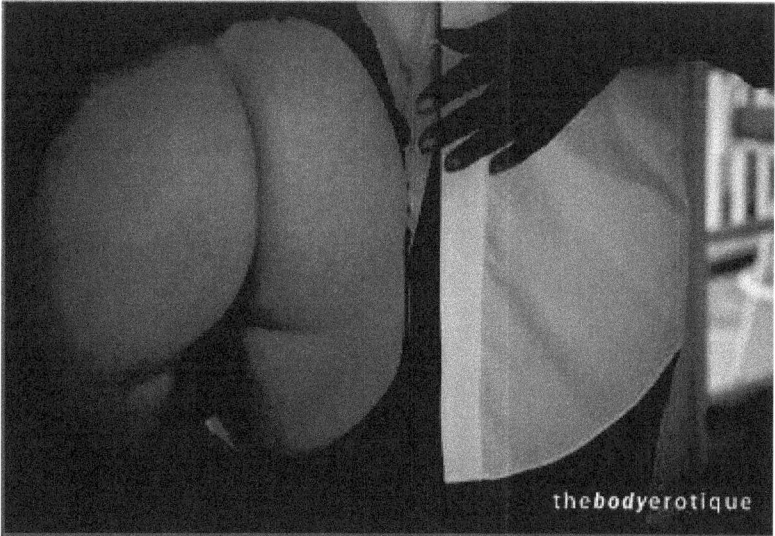

thebodyerotique

I've been called a "Risk Taker" by a twelve year old and damn if he wasn't right. But I'm a simple girl—I do something nice because people do nice things for me, and the back and forth of giving builds friendship, trust, love, and the like. So of course, I went blindly into my passion for play, and avoided thinking through the "what could go wrong?" scenarios. My plan: teach my new lover about fire play in a nice ménage-a-trois scene. I can't help it; I crave memories more than fantasies.

When the play started I could hear myself repeat the words of caution, patience, and safety with hair and clothing and burning. I knew one touch would lead to another and then another until the flames of passion lapped up and grasped our throats waiting for the quench of satiation to take us over.

I could see my hands move across her body as they had hundreds of bodies before. I could see the skin bristle and rise to the touch and crave the caress of my hand against it, calming it and releasing the pleasure to the surface of her body. When the flame, my hand, and her skin met, there was alchemy and magic to be savored.

But rubbing alcohol is still 30% water and the flames of passion I lit were now gone. The 70% that kept a glittery glow on everything was gone, and I was introduced to the death of infatuation. My flames slipped from me and fell to the floor not able to catch the energy loop that would have kept us spinning higher and higher till orgasms were simply the cherries on top. There was just water left.

What had changed? What crack in the universe let this nightmare scenario befall? The answer came with the oxytocin withdrawals. We are primates of tradition. Religion and division clearly spoke our *fears and goals* for the evening when we said, "I don't want to hurt anyone" followed by, "I don't want to feel like sloppy seconds."

Guess what happened? That's right, we both got what we asked for! How so? As with most computers there's a glitch somewhere, and you know for us humans, there are a few glitches in our programming. Otherwise your dick would be bigger and your boobs perkier, right? One of the big glitches is this: <u>The planet is designed to meet all your needs and pleasures</u>. So when a negative command statement includes a "don't" or "not'", the computer that we call the Universe, Hal or God throws out the negative and gives you what you ask for.

Damn, I wish I would have known that growing up. So I hope you get this: If you speak your fear, you will get it. Speak your desire instead. It's that simple, now go change the world.

The Hunt for Real Human Experiences (RHEs)

I'm on a quest for RHEs not experienced before. And if they're good, I'd like to do them again.

A few items on my Kinky Intention List:

* Mile High Club Member—Anyone really done it in the airplane bathroom?

* Three Nights with a Fijian Lover?

* An Honoring?Double, Triple and maybe Quad Penetration Scene?

* Philanthropic/Humiliation/Financial Domination Power Play Scene

* Model my Heroines—(Some of my shit is too kinky even for ya'll)?

* Sing in Paris?

* See the Sex Caves in Ajanta, India?

* Produce a Tibetan Monks Bukakke Scene?

* Build my human lazy susan?performance piece

* Find humans with who I am in alignment, to work with and love

Don't atta boy me just yet or I'll trick my brain into thinking I've already done all of this. Of course, I welcome your encouragement, but I don't want to be lazy on these little masturbatory fantasies that I want to make into memories!

There Ought to Be a Law

Requiring Women to ask for what they want sexually. We have no problem saying, "Why don't you love me?" "What's wrong with me?" "When are you going to call?"

But we often fall short of asking, "When will I get my orgasms? And how long will it take you to satisfy me?" *I can get off without you, but I want to get off with you.* Asking for what you want gets you a lot more quickly to getting what you want. My partner always says, "You don't ask, you don't get."

So when I lifted my head from the computer and said, "Honey, let's fool around," and he closed the lid on his laptop and smiled at me, I said, "Good Night Gentle Kinkster, I'm off practicing what I preach!"

Check out my TIT's

My Tits: Cool tattoos, right? The story is this: I had 44DDs and got tired of them, so I had them cut off. But I hated the scars, so I covered them up. Then I lost 120 lbs. and lost my tits. Now, I want new ones and I'm taking donations here.

My Ten Intention Tips (TITs) are tools for you to use to manifest what you want in your life. I love researching in so many disciplines that it's all starting to come together. And, you're kinky, and I like that about you.

Why do you need both types of TITS? Because you have too much porn in your life and not enough sex. That's why you're here, reading and not sexing. Constantly teasing our bodies without pleasing them makes us

Republicans or religious zealots. Either way, we become frustrated people. We should be having orgasms every other day for optimal health. That's what Dr. Oz says, and I believe Oprah's TV Doc, don't you?

Still, we will have to work to get through your hang-ups, insecurities, disinterested partners, remote locations, and the like to get healthy.

If you need the fantasy sustainers of porn to keep you alive then please stay alive! My TITs will help you start working on your real goals. There is a way to get there; you just have to find the keys to open the lock. My TITs and hopefully my other tits will inspire you to do just that.

From Lynne McTaggart's book, *The Intention Experiment,* I learned how to manifest my intentions, goals, dreams, and desires. It's been fun, ya'll. I missed *The Secret* when that came out. It was too woo-woo for me. I needed research and science and McTaggart's work fed that.

TEN INTENTIONS TIPS

TIT #1

Frame your intention in the positive. Avoid the use of negative phrases. Don't say what you don't want; the universe is designed to give you what you want, so it cancels out the negative statement and gives you what you've just asked for. For example:

Negative intention: "I don't want to make minimum wage."

Positive Reframe: "I want to make $_____ hourly/monthly/annually."

TIT #2

Start with your highest good first. "I want to graduate from this life by completing all that I am here to learn and accomplish, with honors!"

TIT #3

Sigh into gratitude. This is not thought based, but from the lower chakras—heart/emotion and below. Close your eyes and go into the black space of your core. If you are unhappy or troubled, you will feel the ache. Send love into that ache and begin healing and closing the wounds that have occurred. Learn to be a salve for your own body. Look at that which aches and simply love it, forgive it, nourish it back. Be a good parent for yourself.

TIT #4

For 17 seconds steadily hold the vision of what you desire in your mind's eye. Let the rest of your senses follow the visual of your desire.

TIT #5

Be careful of the auto loop. Your brain has a mechanism that makes it second-guess its own intuition. Recognize the difference between the original impulse and the secondary one.

TIT #6

Listen to the free FinerMinds.com video: The Five Steps of Manifesting.

TIT #7

Create rituals for yourself to positively reinforce good thoughts, behaviors, and results you want.

TIT #8

Don't speak your fear! It will manifest. Remember: the universe does not hear a negative, which is a glitch in the system, so don't trip over the wire. After all, the earth is not perfect.

TIT #9

Evil and good are equal, the same as positive and negative. It seems that way sometimes because we create a sharp picture of evil, and good is often nebulous.

TIT #10

Your words are your key. The bible gives us a clue. My paraphrasing of Genesis, Chapter 1: "In the beginning there was nothing but void, and the spirit hovering. Then came the words: 'Let there be...'" Seven days later somebody manifested a planet. Pretty cool, eh?

Mother Hubbard

Courtesy of J. Michael Walker

I was home on a Saturday night with a cold. My beloved was out playing with a cute little vixen, tying her up and making her cum over and over again. Life sucks!

But other than the cold I had no complaints. My client from last night tipped generously, and I got home before midnight. Though being out in the cold accelerated my health problems, it also gave me a chance to take a call from a young man nervously making his first call to a Pro Domme.

What a delight to coax the next generation to explore their kinky side and expand their own horizons of what can be. I know my Pro sisters would say I'm not being tough enough on the young pup, but you remember the cliche, "the hooker with a heart of gold"? I couldn't help it, I don't remember ever having someone I could call and ask about a session of play to explore my dirty little thoughts.

Today, even in America, we can explore and try out what fits our life-styles. Try it on for size and see if it feels good. I reminded him that I would be nice until he pissed me off. I find I'm striking a balance between Mother Hubbard and sadistic sensualist.

Sweep Me Back Under the Rug

I never thought I would regret the day the Internet brought kink to the world, but I am there. That dirty little secret we kept under the rug is now out in the open and growing like a weed. In my early days of kink, we did not gossip or judge the quality of their play or protocol. We didn't gossip online or at munches because we were just grateful to have a friend to share with our lifestyle secret. One we could relax for a change and know we were safe.

But those days are gone. The baggage we muck about in our vanilla lives is creeping into the leather community. We are comfortable, so we make time to judge and turn our noses up at the kink or fetish that is not our own. We are sadly even to the point of sexism and racism in the leather lifestyle. We were the last outlaws but, as outlaws are known to do, we have turned on each other.

I understand how it happened, but I wonder, where it will lead? I saw an ad for the Stockroom in our local weekly LA mag-a-paper: "BDSM is the new Black." Oh my, now we are trendy. Something in me wants to shout "THIS CAN'T BE GOOD!" I guess my biggest fear is that we will become passé.' With the rush for play to get edgier and edgier I wonder if we will need snuff films to get off? Surely not? Please, someone tell me they still find pleasure in creating orgasms, beautiful moans of pleasure and Top/bottom spaces.

I am feeling like an old fuddy-duddy when I think and long for the good old days of kink, when every new kinkling out of the box wasn't trying to make their own floggers and sell them, planning their get-rich-quick scheme. Or to have to read about the travails of ProDommes being written about in national conservative columns. (See Dr. Susie Albright for Fox News). Did you hear the one about the Domme who had the breath play scene go terribly wrong? Or the Top who left his girl for another sub, or the one about the sub who spread lies about her Dom to gain community pity when she wanted to end the relationship? You name it, we've done something to someone. I say *we*, because if I have listened to the gossip, I'm a part of the problem.

I guess that's why I have refused to take on anything more than play partners. I didn't want the stickiness of relationship with another partner. Wife was the one job I wanted to keep. Though I fantasized about two hot bodies to share my bed with, the reality of another snoring head and the mess that comes with it was sobering. And we all got to sleep sometime!

So now my play is just about play on my terms. I want to go to my sandbox, aka dungeon, and play, giggle, show off, and then go home to my bed. Sweep my personal life back under the rug where it belongs. The olde dark dungeon just ain't what it used to be.

The Bucket List

A comment on one of my Fetlife pics got me to thinking. A gentle-man mentioned that my scene was on his bucket list. You know, that list we are supposed to make before we kick the bucket. Well, last year a wonderful submissive woman I knew suddenly died. Her death was the first time someone I personally knew in the lifestyle submitted to that final Master, the Grim Reaper.

It got me to thinking again about that inevitable path I must pass through and what's on my bucket list. Surprisingly, it's pretty short, be-cause my Aunt told me years ago that I had lived my life backwards. I had traveled around the world (three times) and now all I had left was forty years of work. That was a hell of an eye opener!

I changed my life from then on and decided to break it up in-tosegments: on my own at sixteen to nineteen I went to college(s). At twenty, I quit college, and sex and became a celibate missionary from the ages of twenty to thirty-two. Yeah, really, and I got the handmade quilts to prove I spent hours in bed with absolutely nothing else to do!

In my 30s I rebuilt a career; 40s brought a marriage & family because my eggs were screaming, "We're dying here, do something!" Then, the last half of my forties, the Big C dominated all decision making. After a couple hard sharp turns, I found my second wind. With it came a burst of testosterone to grow the pair of balls I needed to pull off being single and fifty. But as my Great Aunt Gertrude said, "Nothing beats a failure like a try." You learn to go for broke.

My Second Wind—I remember a news story that said after a certain income level, money won't make you happy. That was a relief and it got me off the Ferris wheel of chasing money. I'm a grateful, lucky gal, so much I don't do affirmations anymore, I just live them.

Learning the language of manifesting intentions has given me a better set of keys to unlock the mysterious universe with. Sounds woo-woo right? You know, overly spiritual and stuff? But good news, I got the science and it's sexy good news for us hedonists. My mission on this planet is to share with you what I've learned.

Thirdly, I want my libido and my body to always be in sync. Let me explain. As I get older, I've learned that my sex drive is still stronger than ever, however, my aching _____ (fill in the blank with any of the following)…

Back Arms Tooth Feet Legs Head Eyes Ears Boobs

This really caused me a lot of frustration. I wanted to get my groove on and can't because of the focus on post-chemo pain. So then I wanted to hit somebody and release my tension and frustration but there was never a masochist around when I needed one. Finally, I had to remind myself, "Don't hit angry". And all I needed was a strong orgasm. It's that frustration of culture, religion, politics, and job that kept my legs closed and frustrated. Really, what good am I doing the planet with that attitude? So for my last item on my bucket list, I want to go out having the best fucking orgasm ever to welcome me to the next life! Just like David Carradine, sans the rope.

And finally, I like this little ditty my former-hubby shared with me once:

THE SENILITY PRAYER
Grant me the senility to forget the people I never liked anyway,
The good fortune to run into the ones I do, and
The eyesight to tell the difference

What's on your list?

What's Next?

meek

Mastermind for Erotic Entrepreneurs and Kinksters

Because the meek shall inherit the earth.

Ever felt rejected by business colleagues because you were in the Adult industry?

Do you have the professional support for your sex positive business needs?

Are you manifesting the results you want in your personal life?

Are you ready to level-up your business to the next stage?

Then it's time you become a **meek.**

meek is a mastermind group for erotic and kink friendly entrepreneurs and small business owners like you. **meeks** have made their passion their profession and are ready to accelerate their success.

What makes you a **meek** is your ability to be in alignment with a sex positive viewpoint. It makes you less judgemental, open to new ideas, and you have a broader scope of your purpose on the planet. I like that about you. **meek** gives its members the opportunity to combine industry focused growth for their business along with personal development support for themselves.

"Seek the counsel of [those] who will tell you the truth about yourself, even if it hurts you to hear it. Mere commendation will not bring the improvement you need." Napoleon Hill

You will learn ***Intentional Manifesting*** for your business and personal success through the extensive research in quantum physics from Lynne

McTaggart's work, *The Intention Experiment* and *The Bond*. **meeks** are committed and ready to level-up their lives. **meek** is about aligning the spiritual, intellectual, emotional, instinctual, and sexual centers of the body for personal and professional development.

"It's the actions that follow the intentions that deliver the manifestation results you desire." Phyllis-Serene

meeks come together monthly to mastermind and set their manifesting intentions through small group business coaching, training, networking, marketing, and invitations for exclusive networks with like-minded sex positive professionals.

"No two minds ever come together without, thereby, creating a third, invisible intangible force which may be likened to a third mind." Napoleon Hill

Your **meek** resources will be in your life supporting, challenging, and believing in YOU, your goals and desires. For this reason, applicants to join **meeks** are carefully selected.. I select members who are ready to *get in alignment* with their professional and personal lives.

Getting in alignment is the basis for the **meeks**. It brings together the five elements important for overall healthy living:

Spirituality
Intellect
Emotions
Instinct
Sexuality

You will learn how to get in alignment individually and in relationship with others. Meshing these areas first takes individuals like you who

126

are comfortable with their sexuality. There is no other program in the world that combines all these elements in a coaching program.

meek is the culmination of my two passions in life: learning and sharing. My passion for personal growth and sexuality coincided together at the age of five when I discovered Japanese Bondage while living abroad. The excitement of discovery combined with sexuality fused within me and thus became my first fetish.

My professional career has included managing a Federal Empowerment Zone, a youth and adult entrepreneurship education nonprofit. I owned an executive recruiting firm, spent three years as a national motivational speaker, and am the author of four books on career mapping and online dating.

I am fortunate to have been raised with a healthy sexuality, which has continued into my adult life: privately practicing BDSM as a professional, yet open in my relationships. At fifty, I decided it was time to *come out* of the kink closet. The Universe gave me a present when I won the title of Southern California Leather Woman 2010.

In that year of service I enjoyed reconnecting with amazing, grounded entrepreneurs. Today, I'm thrilled to be able to share with you what I've learned and profited from.

What's in it for the meek -

Get advice from experienced professional - Get the focused attention for your business needs and the resources from industry experience professionals.

Manifest your goals - Get the keys to unlock the manifesting power on your own.

Network with your peers - Get advice by posting questions and sharing resources.

Increase your business knowledge - Listen, when it's convenient for you, to educational topics relevant to your industry.

Sell your stuff - Free ad for your product or service in the Erotic Entrepreneurs Directory.

Make Trades - Barter and trade product and services with peers.

Stay Connected - Learn how to get access to invitation only social networks.

Encouragement - Make friends with people who get you and want to be in alignment with you.

meek is a virtual group that meets online and through Google groups. All educational calls are recorded for access anytime to members. For more details go to www.serenesin.com

Thank you for taking the time to invest in yourself and your work with this one **meek** step. That's living in alignment.

"Live each day like it's your last, and learn like you will live forever." - *Mahatma Gandhi*

Resources

Serene Reading List

Fiction:

Rice, Anne: <u>The Beauty Series</u> and <u>Exit to Eden</u>
Antoniou, Laura: <u>The MarketPlace, The Slave, The Trainer, The Academy, By Her Subdued</u>

Non-Fiction:

Baldwin, Guy: <u>Ties That Bind</u>
Jacques Trevor: <u>On The Safe Edge: A Manual for SM Play</u>
Service:
Mumford, Susan: <u>The Complete Guide to Massage</u>
Abernathy Christina: <u>Training With Miss Abernathy: A Workbook for Erotic Slaves and Their Owners</u>

Personal Growth:

Enneagrams: Rohr, Richard: <u>Discovering The Ennegram</u>
Chinese Horoscope: Lau, Theodora: <u>The Handbook of Chinese Horoscopes</u>
Western Horoscope: Goodman, Linda: <u>Love Signs</u>
Life Purpose/Numerology: Millman, Dan: <u>The Life You Were Born To Live</u>

Quantum Physics:

Lynne McTaggart, <u>The Intention Experiment</u> & <u>The Bond</u>

Relationships:

Esther Perel, <u>Mating in Captivity</u>

Dossie Easton, Catherine A. Liszt, <u>When Someone You Love is Kinky</u>

End Notes

[1] "Vanilla" or "Vanilla Sex"— referring to conventional life and sexual behavior.

[2] Conn, Peter Pear S. Buck, A Cultural Biography. 1st Cambridge, Cambridge University Press, 1996.

[3] Owen AD, Hayward RD, Koenig HG, Steffens DC, Payne ME (2011) Religious Factors and Hippocampal Atrophy in Late Life. PLoS ONE 6(3): e17006. doi:10.1371/journal.pone.0017006